DATE DUE

Meenaz Shams

Reading Difficulties in Children

A study of dyslexia in the mainstream, multilingual
context of Pakistan

LAP LAMBERT Academic Publishing

371. 9144 SHA

Impressum/Imprint (nur für Deutschland/only for Germany)
Bibliografische Information der Deutschen Nationalbibliothek: Die Deutsche Nationalbibliothek verzeichnet diese Publikation in der Deutschen Nationalbibliografie; detaillierte bibliografische Daten sind im Internet über http://dnb.d-nb.de abrufbar.
Alle in diesem Buch genannten Marken und Produktnamen unterliegen warenzeichen-, marken- oder patentrechtlichem Schutz bzw. sind Warenzeichen oder eingetragene Warenzeichen der jeweiligen Inhaber. Die Wiedergabe von Marken, Produktnamen, Gebrauchsnamen, Handelsnamen, Warenbezeichnungen u.s.w. in diesem Werk berechtigt auch ohne besondere Kennzeichnung nicht zu der Annahme, dass solche Namen im Sinne der Warenzeichen- und Markenschutzgesetzgebung als frei zu betrachten wären und daher von jedermann benutzt werden dürften.

Coverbild: www.ingimage.com

Verlag: LAP LAMBERT Academic Publishing GmbH & Co. KG
Dudweiler Landstr. 99, 66123 Saarbrücken, Deutschland
Telefon +49 681 3720-310, Telefax +49 681 3720-3109
Email: info@lap-publishing.com

Approved by: Karachi, Aga Khan University - Institute for Educational Development, Diss., 2000

Herstellung in Deutschland:
Schaltungsdienst Lange o.H.G., Berlin
Books on Demand GmbH, Norderstedt
Reha GmbH, Saarbrücken
Amazon Distribution GmbH, Leipzig
ISBN: 978-3-8454-2275-6

Imprint (only for USA, GB)
Bibliographic information published by the Deutsche Nationalbibliothek: The Deutsche Nationalbibliothek lists this publication in the Deutsche Nationalbibliografie; detailed bibliographic data are available in the Internet at http://dnb.d-nb.de.
Any brand names and product names mentioned in this book are subject to trademark, brand or patent protection and are trademarks or registered trademarks of their respective holders. The use of brand names, product names, common names, trade names, product descriptions etc. even without a particular marking in this works is in no way to be construed to mean that such names may be regarded as unrestricted in respect of trademark and brand protection legislation and could thus be used by anyone.

Cover image: www.ingimage.com

Publisher: LAP LAMBERT Academic Publishing GmbH & Co. KG
Dudweiler Landstr. 99, 66123 Saarbrücken, Germany
Phone +49 681 3720-310, Fax +49 681 3720-3109
Email: info@lap-publishing.com

Printed in the U.S.A.
Printed in the U.K. by (see last page)
ISBN: 978-3-8454-2275-6

06010

TABLE OF CONTENTS

This research study is a Masters' dissertation submitted for the degree of
M.Ed. - Master in Education (Teacher Education) at the
Aga Khan University – Institute for Educational Development,
Karachi, Pakistan.

August, 2000.

DEDICATION

THIS PIECE OF RESEARCH WORK
IS DEDICATED TO THE CHILDREN ALL OVER THE WORLD
WHO ARE FACING READING DIFFICULTIES
AND ARE LABELED AS
"READING DISABLED" OR "DYSLEXIC"
WITH A HOPE THAT ONE DAY
THEIR LEARNING PROBLEMS WILL BE UNDERSTOOD
AND THEIR DIFFERENT LEARNING STYLES
WILL BE CATERED FOR
BY THE SCHOOLS,
TEACHERS AND
PARENTS…

ACKNOWLEDGMENT

I would like to thank several people whose support and advice led to the completion of this research work. First of all, I would like to thank my supervisor Dr. Fauzia Shamim for her scholarly guidance and encouragement that contributed significantly to the completion of this research study.

My Special thanks to Dr. Gordon MacLeod, Dr. Tashmin Khamis, Dr. Debbie Kramer Roy, Ms. Azra Naseem, Ms. Farah Shivji, Ms. Atiya Hussain, Ms. Fauzia Qureshi, and all faculty and staff of the Aga Khan University – Institute for Educational Development for the guidance and support they gave throughout this research work.

My extra ordinary thanks and gratitude to Ms. Erum Maqbool, who as a resource person, supported me throughout this study with her professional input.

My heartiest thanks and gratitude to my friends and classmates, especially Anisa, Munira, Saima, Ruth, Elizabeth, Amir, Fred, Peter, Rahim and all my colleagues for giving me moral support and sharing their knowledge and wisdom. They were also a source of inspiration and motivation when my research study was refocused.

It has been the cooperation and enthusiasm of many other people, which has enabled the completion of this study. In this respect, special thanks to all dear children and teachers who participated in this research and without whose co-operation, the study would have not been possible. I am grateful to Ms. Gohar Karim and Ms. Shaheen Meraj, who kindly assisted in proof reading and editing of my work.

Last, my deep thanks to my beloved husband, Shams and all my family members whose love, care, support and prayers have made it possible for me to complete my research work. All this has been possible due to Allah's benevolence and I pray that He further guides me into every step of my professional career, Ameen.

ABBREVIATIONS

CO   Classroom Observation of Reading lessons

IST   Interview with Specialist Reading Teacher

ITT   Interview with Trained Reading Teacher

IUT   Interview with Untrained Reading Teacher

RO   Remedial Reading Observation

AKU   Aga Khan University

SON   School of Nursing

IED   Institute for Educational Development

M.Ed.   Master in Education (Teacher Education)

IPC   Integrated Primary Curriculum

SPM   Standard Progressive Matrices

SORT   Slosson Oral Reading Test

WRAT-R   Wide Range Achievement Test - Revised

6

Chapter One

INTRODUCTION

Reading is vital to all learning, as it is the base on which literacy exists. It plays an important role in the child's learning process, as it is one of the key ways of learning. It is an essential skill to be acquired by children, if they want to function normally, acquire knowledge and lead an effective life in the world as a successful learner. It is the base of all the learning processes as it helps in independent learning. It is one of the basic skills that influence other skills like writing, spelling, vocabulary, pronunciation, etc. as it plays a major role in the learning process of the children. Unless they are able to read, they will not understand and comprehend the text. Therefore reading and understanding go together as it is makes the learning process more meaningful and effective. Research shows that some children have problems in learning to read, which if not identified and catered for at an early stage, lead to life long reading difficulties that hinder the child's learning process.

Background and Context of the Study

As a student I was a very slow reader. I faced problems in understanding the text I read. I sometimes used to read paragraphs and sentences again and again in order to understand what the writer was trying to convey. I never proceeded reading a text if I did not understand what I had already read. May be this was because of my slow reading speed or perhaps I had poor decoding and comprehension skills. To compound that, my teacher usually asked me to read aloud in front of my classmates, as she knew my reading speed was very slow. Perhaps she wanted to keep track of my progress. But while reading aloud, I used to concentrate more on the pronunciation of words than the meaning of what I was reading. After I finished reading, she would usually ask me questions to see whether I had understood the text or not. But I faced problems in comprehending the text read, as I could not concentrate on both pronunciation and comprehension simultaneously. My teacher knew that I was a slow reader and had problems in understanding the text, but never tried to help me with my reading problems. In this way she would have at least raised my self-esteem and confidence by giving me individual attention, guided and supported me while reading, etc. That, I think, would have helped me overcome my problem. Instead she used to refer to me as 'slow' and 'dull.'

Later, as a primary English teacher, during my 15 years of teaching life, I also experienced children with different reading problems in my class. Since as a student, I had been facing problems in reading, I was very conscious about my students' reading problems and tried to help and facilitate them. Usually these reading problems were skipping words while reading, and being unable to pronounce words they had already been taught. In addition, they faced comprehension difficulties, reversals of sounds/letters in reading the words, had slow reading speed and repeated words rather than reading the next coming word in the text, etc. Owing to my student-life experiences, I was very conscious about my responsibility to help these children with their reading difficulties. But unfortunately, I was unaware of the causes and the remedial teaching strategies, which could cater to and help them in overcoming their reading problems. I used to discuss it with my colleagues and they used to give reasons like children being careless, inattentive, less motivated, etc. They used to label these children as 'weak' and 'dull' students because of their low performance level. They even used to blame their family background and parents' illiteracy for that. But deep in my heart, I knew that there was much more to it than that, so I used to facilitate them by helping them to read. Besides I counseled the children as well as the parents in order to help the children in their learning process.

I became aware of children's learning difficulties when I was transferred to the pre-primary section. The head teacher of the pre-primary was Montessori trained and had also attended a training course on how to deal with children with learning difficulties and therefore used to implement remedial strategies for overcoming children's learning difficulties. Being the deputy head, I was also involved in the planning and implementation of remedial strategies to help children with learning difficulties. The more I became involved in this work, the more I developed an interest in knowing and exploring about the same. I worked there for one year and then I was selected for the M.Ed. program at IED. After joining the program, whenever I got an opportunity to read,

8

I utilized my time in reading about special educational needs and learning difficulties. This, in turn, created awareness which led me to explore more about children's different learning styles and learning difficulties especially related to English language i.e. reading, writing, spelling, speaking and listening.

Statement of the Problem

Children in primary schools in Pakistan do have reading difficulties. These difficulties vary among different individual students. Through whatever I have read, understood and experienced, I have come to know that if these difficulties are not catered for at an early stage, then the children's process of learning is hindered, as these reading difficulties may create difficulties in other areas and skills like writing, spelling, etc. But for this, teachers should have awareness, knowledge and understanding of the problem as well as skills and strategies to help children overcome their reading difficulties.

Purpose and Significance of the Study

The aim of conducting this research study is to identify children's reading difficulties in a bi-lingual or multi-lingual context like Pakistan, and to explore ways of raising teacher's awareness to help these children with their reading difficulties at the primary level. The study findings also highlight the possibilities and challenges, which could be encountered by the teachers in investigating the prevailing reading difficulties in children and catering for the same, by using specific remedial strategies. This research study has given me insights by defining my future role as a teacher and a teacher educator, in addressing the issues and challenges encountered while exploring this research topic and collecting relevant data. This in turn has helped me to recommend suggestions for that particular school context, where the needs analysis study was conducted. This will also facilitate my future work with the teachers in my own school context to raise their awareness level and help them in identifying children's reading difficulties and use suitable and appropriate remedial strategies to facilitate children's learning process.

Research has shown many studies on children's learning difficulties. Through the result of these studies, remedial programs have been developed for dealing with children's specific learning difficulties. These research studies have been conducted on both native and non-native speakers of English language. However, only few research studies have been conducted, in the area of reading difficulties or dyslexia in Pakistan. In Pakistan, English is either taught as a second, third or foreign language. Moreover, very few people are aware of children's reading difficulties in our context. Recently a few people have specialized in specific areas of learning difficulties and have opened institutions for dealing with children's difficulties effectively. But these institutions are few in number and therefore their remedial treatment programs are very expensive. These institutions also offer training courses for teachers but again these are also very expensive. But in the government and other private schools, teachers do not have much awareness of the learning difficulties faced by the children. Even if these teachers identify students with reading difficulties, they cannot refer them to remedial centres, since the parents are unable to afford the high fees of these institutions.

The importance of this study is that it has been carried out in a school context where English is taught as a second language, but is often the third language for many children. The aim is to find out whether children have reading difficulties and/or language difficulties in reading English language. Therefore the significance of the study lies in the identification of children's reading difficulties in English as a second language and that makes the study contextually relevant. In addition, the study aims to explore the facilities available to deal with children's reading difficulties. The research findings would also help me in planning and implementing remedial strategies to facilitate my future role as a teacher and teacher educator in my own school, where children are learning English as a second or third language. Thus, the significance of the study is not just to find out reading difficulties in children but to find out the possible facilities available for a school of a middle level clientele and to what extent are the reading difficulties common throughout the different school contexts and to what extent are these reading difficulties addressed highlighting the issues encountered in that particular school context, or in Pakistan.

This study was divided into two phases. The first phase comprised of a needs analysis in a primary school context to find teachers' level of awareness of children's reading difficulties. For this, language teachers were interviewed and their reading classes were observed. However, in order to identify reading difficulties in children, a sample of 21 students from class V was randomly selected and assessed using standardized tests. The reason for the needs analysis was to try and find out if teachers are aware, and things are being done then what could be done in future to build upon that. And if nothing is being done, than at least things could be started. In the second phase, I visited the remedial centres, which cater for the needs of children having reading difficulties and interviewed some of the specialist professional reading teachers and also observed their remedial teaching sessions. This was done to explore how these remedial centres identify and remediate children's reading difficulties. The trained reading teachers working in selected schools, identified by these centers, were interviewed to explore how the schools can accommodate and cater for the children's difficulties in reading. This gave insights about ways for raising awareness level among the teachers and recommending an action plan, which could be carried out in the sample school. Therefore, the aim of the study was to try and understand certain mechanisms that could be put in place for the particular school where the needs analysis study was conducted because that is the main area of interest as it is my own school. Therefore, the information gathered in the exploration phase would help to enhance the understanding of the problem. Consequently a program could be instituted in future at the school level, or a project at the system level to raise awareness among the teachers that would in turn help them to cater for children's reading difficulties.

Assumptions of the Study

The assumptions of the study were:
➢ Children have reading difficulties.
➢ Children's reading difficulties differ in nature and are due to different causes.
➢ Early interventions help children to overcome their reading difficulties.
➢ Most of the teachers are not aware of these difficulties and therefore do not cater for

this.

> Even if teachers are aware of them, they are not trained enough to implement remedial reading strategies to help children overcome these difficulties.

Research Questions

The following are the research questions:

Main research question

"How can teachers help children with reading difficulties in English at the primary level in the multi-lingual context of Pakistan?"

Subsidiary questions

1. What types of reading difficulties do primary children have in ESL classrooms in Pakistan?
2. What are their causes?
3. To what extent are children's reading difficulties catered for by the teachers and how?
4. What remedial strategies are being used to help children overcome their reading difficulties?
5. What are the possibilities and challenges for teachers in dealing with children's reading difficulties in the multi-lingual context of Pakistan?

Defining Key Terms

Reading difficulties

The reading process consists of skills, which include recognizing printed words, determining the meaning of words, phrases, and sentences to comprehend the meaning of the text read. Reading difficulties basically involve a failure either to recognize or to comprehend written material, which hinders the learning process of the child. The difficulties children face in learning to read, block their access to a wide range of information acquisition. Therefore, the term 'reading difficulties' is understood to be both decoding and comprehension difficulties. The decoding difficulties are problems related to the recognition of words. In other words these are problems related in mapping between the letters and their sounds, which can be caused by perceptual deficits, phonological processing deficits, memory deficits, etc. Whereas the comprehension difficulties are problems related to the meaning of what is recognized, which can be at times a result of having poor decoding skills, which hinders in the understanding of the written text. These difficulties are observed due to the inefficiencies of the hidden cognitive components that are involved in processing the written input. In short, reading difficulties create a vicious circle, which presents an illustration of the problems that may be experienced and an indication that, with help, motivation and progress can be improved (Dockrell & McShane, 1992).

Pollock and Waller (1997) explain the term 'reading difficulties,' as used also in this research study in the following way:

> Reading difficulties may manifest themselves initially with the actual mechanics of reading but, even if these are mastered, there may be problems with comprehension. It is not unusual for a child to attain a reasonable level of accuracy in decoding words and to have difficulty in extracting the meaning from text, perhaps because his concentration is centered on the phonological process. (p.36)

For the purpose of this research study, decoding skills were focused as the study conducted was only looking at the primary level children who are at the beginning level of learning English. Therefore, the term 'reading difficulties' used in this research study only refers to reading difficulties of decoding types.

Chapter Two
LITERATURE REVIEW

Many children experience difficulties in learning. According to the U.S. Department of Education's Individuals with Disabilities Act (IDEA) of 1990, a learning disability is:

> A disorder in one or more of the basic psychological processes involved in understanding or in using language, spoken or written, which may manifest itself in an imperfect ability to listen, think, speak, read, write, spell, or to do mathematical calculations. The term includes such conditions as perceptual handicaps, brain injury, minimal brain dysfunction, dyslexia, and developmental aphasia. The term does not include children who have learning problems that are primarily the result of visual, hearing, or motor handicaps, of mental retardation, or environmental, cultural, or economic disadvantage (Lokerson, 1992b, p.2).

The term 'learning difficulties' or 'learning disabilities' (LD) refers to all individuals who have some neurological impairment that mixes up the signals between the senses and the brain. By definition, children who are LDs have average or above average intelligence, but they experience problems when their brain receives stimuli from their senses. The 'disability' or 'difficulty' lies in the area of the brain where processing problems occur. Research studies show that these problems occur because these children have differences in the functioning of the brain as compared to other children of the same age and therefore they have problems in learning things conventionally. Also these problems vary in children and thus can be dealt with different remedial strategies.

The terms like 'learning disabilities,' 'learning disorders,' 'learning problems,' (Leadbetter & Leadbetter, 1993), 'learning difficulties,' 'special learning difficulties,' 'learning differences,' 'special way of learning' or 'different way of learning' (Pollock & Waller, 1997) are used synonymously by the authors and researchers. The differences in the interchangeable use of these terms are mostly related to the perspective it defines, whether negative or positive, but usually they are discussed under the wide umbrella of 'special educational needs' referring to the children's 'learning problems'. The understanding one gets from these definitions seems to explain that an individual can be born with a learning disability which can be physical, mental or emotional, but the learning difficulties could be experiences due to a particular disability and not as an innate incapability. Hence it is understood that there is a slight line drawn between disabilities and difficulties and therefore, there might be an overlap in the use of these terms.

Every year, there is an increase in the number of students found to have learning difficulties, yet many of these students are not properly diagnosed, as it is a 'hidden disability' (Lokerson, 1992a), which sometimes is undetected until either academic or social problems occur. Children with learning difficulties may show these signs in one or more areas. The signs may be obvious depending upon the age and intelligence of the child and the ability of the child to compensate for the leaning problem. He further states that children are often quite efficient in hiding difficulties that might reveal the presence of learning disabilities or they might be unaware that these difficulties may be the cause of the problem.

It is understood from the widely accepted definitions of learning disabilities or difficulties over a number of years that learning disabilities/difficulties implicitly reflect a significant discrepancy at the performance level between the child's overall intellectual ability and his/her accepted or displayed level of academic achievement. According to Lokerson (1992b), some definitions specify an intellectual range and others add a concept of discrepancy between potential and achievement and sometimes they quantify the discrepancy using the test scores. But again the deficits are unique to the individuals and may occur across the life span and also they vary in the nature of severity. They also can affect one or more of the child's abilities to acquire and use his/her skills in the areas of listening, speaking, reading, writing, reasoning and mathematics (Pumfrey & Delliot, 1993). According to Lerner (1989):

Research studies show that although students with learning disabilities have difficulties in many areas of learning, but 80 percent of it, is identified relatively to poor reading, which highlights it to be the major reported academic problem (Lyon, 1985; Kirk & Elkins, 1975). It is important, therefore, that teachers of children with reading difficulties should be well grounded in the concepts and methodologies of reading. (p.348)

Recent research studies also show that 80-85% of students with learning disabilities have their basic deficits in language and reading. Studies also highlight that reading difficulty, such as dyslexia, or problems with reading and language, are the most commonly occurring learning difficulties (Antonoff, 1998; TeachEach, 1997). Specific learning disabilities (SLD) are learning difficulties faced by children in a specific area of learning. As defined by Lokerson (1992a), SLD refers to "a severe difficulty in some aspect of listening, speaking, reading, writing, or spelling, while skills in the other areas are age-appropriate" (p.3), whereas Specific Language Learning Disability (SLLD) is related to specifically language learning areas. This highlights that the reading difficulties can also be placed in the category of specific learning difficulties/ disabilities. Thus a variety of different types of learning disabilities exist in different specific areas and therefore, specialized assessment and teaching assistance is needed to help these children overcome their learning difficulties which would in turn facilitate their learning process effectively.

Reading Difficulties in Children

'Reading difficulties' in the literature has alternatively been used with terms like 'reading retardation,' 'reading disorders,' 'reading problems,' and 'reading disabilities.' The 'reading disabilities' are also defined as reading disorders which are owing to some physical or mental disability or dis-functioning of the brain, or due to some deficiencies which create problems for children while reading. These labels seem to have a negative connotation to give a more positive aspect to, the terms like 'reading difficulties' or 'reading differences' are used nowadays.

Reading difficulty is an inability or difficulty in reading or processing information. As mentioned above, the child having reading difficulties has problems in decoding or in comprehension, or mostly both (CLD, 1997; Turnbull, Turnbull, Shank, Leal, 1999). In the reading process, the word is first decoded into its phonological form, then identified and then the higher-level cognitive functions such as intelligence and vocabulary are used to understand the word's meaning. But in dyslexics, a phonological deficit impairs decoding, thus preventing the reader from using his or her intelligence and vocabulary to get to the word's meaning (Shaywitz, 1996a). According to Shaywitz (1996b), dyslexia is the most common of the learning disorders, conditions that interfere with a normally intelligent child's ability to acquire speech, reading or cognitive skills (p.82). The most common learning difficulty is reading difficulty or dyslexia. Dyslexia is sometimes characterized as a subgroup of reading difficulties and represents a developmental language impairment which during the preschool years is revealed by difficulties in learning spoken language and during the school years, in acquiring word recognition, spelling skills and reading comprehension skills (CLD, 1997; Turnbull, Turnbull, Shank, Leal, 1999). It is a type of difficulty in which children fail to master basic processes, such as letter recognition and sound blending, despite adequate intelligence and educational opportunities. These are usually related to the auditory-linguistic deficits, or visual-spatial deficits, or mixed deficits. Children, who have auditory-linguistic deficits, exhibit a poor auditory sequential memory span, blending and discrimination difficulties, sound confusion, bizarre spelling problems and sequencing problems. With visual-spatial deficits, children have poor visual sequential memory, visual discrimination and directional problems, difficulties in spelling words that are phonetically irregular, visual analysis, synthesis difficulties and spatial problems. Children with mixed deficits have problems in both language-related areas and visual-spatial areas (TRC Workshop Handout, 2000, p.2-3). According to Antonoff (1998):

> Dyslexia is a neurologically-based, often familial, disorder that interferes with the acquisition and processing of language. Varying in degrees of severity, it is manifested by difficulties in receptive and expressive language, including phonological processing, in reading, writing, spelling, handwriting, and sometimes in arithmetic. Dyslexia is not a result of lack

of motivation, sensory impairment, inadequate instructional or environmental opportunities, or other limiting conditions, but may occur together with these conditions. Although dyslexia is life long, individuals with dyslexia frequently respond successfully to timely and appropriate intervention. (p.1)

Therefore reading difficulties or dyslexia is one of the specific areas of 'learning difficulties' which is caused by individual differences or disabilities to learn to read. Children who are dyslexic do have difficulties with words. These difficulties relate to reading, writing, or spelling of words or sometimes with arithmetic numbers also (Lokerson, 1992a). These children have decoding difficulties and are sometimes labeled as 'dyslexics.' In order to have a positive connotation of the label 'dyslexia,' the recent literature has replaced it with either saying 'a different way of learning' or 'a special way of learning' (Pollock & Waller, 1997; Osmond, 1993).

In literature, terms like 'poor,' 'slow' and 'backward' are also used for readers having reading problems. These readers have reading levels, which fall far bellow their intellectual level (Bryant & Bradley, 1985; Gaffney, 1998). Furthermore, decoding difficulties sometimes result in comprehension difficulties as children having difficulty in learning to decode, process the text word-by-word rather than at the level of phrases and sentences which leads to poor comprehension skills. As Dockrell & McShane (1992) state:

Reading difficulties can be analyzed at two levels: decoding and comprehension. Difficulties reflect inefficiencies in the underlying cognitive components that are involved in processing written input. Comprehension difficulties are sometimes the result of poor decoding skills. In many cases children who have had difficulty in learning to decode, process text on a word-by-word basis rather than at the level of phrases and sentences. This leads to poor comprehension. (p.119)

The research literature on reading difficulties focuses both on decoding and comprehension difficulties faced by children while reading. The decoding problems are related with difficulties in learning to map between letters and sounds. These are due to the inefficiencies of the cognitive components that are involved in processing the written input (Dockrell & McShane, 1992). The nature of these reading difficulties can be mild, moderate or severe (William, 1990; Dockrell & McShane, 1992). Current research indicates that the vast majority of children with dyslexia have phonological core deficits. The severity of the phonological deficits varies across individuals, and children with these deficits have been shown to make significantly less progress in basic word reading skills compared to children with an equivalent IQ (Frost & Emery, 1995). These problems lead the child to misread and mispronounce the words, difficulty in identifying letters and words, improper recognition of phonemes, or lack of awareness of word sounds, rhymes or the sequence of sounds and syllables in words, misarticulating or reversing of letters or words like 'bad,' as 'dad,' 'but,' as 'put,' 'animal,' as 'aminal,' 'sign,' as 'sing,' 'left,' as 'felt,' etc. or omission of letters or words, mostly prefixes and suffixes such as 'unwanted,' as 'wanted,' 'blamed,' as 'blame,' or connector words like 'or,' 'but,' 'and,' etc. stumbling over words, repetition of words or sentences, addition of words, reading and rereading, not understanding what is read, etc. (Vellutino, 1987; Antonoff, 1998; Judah, 1999). These word recognition errors and comprehension difficulties, reading can be frustrating for the children (CLD, 1997; Turnbull, Turnbull, Shank, Leal, 1999). Antonoff (1998), in his research findings, further highlights that a child with dyslexia or other learning disabilities is intelligent, sometimes gifted in certain areas, for e.g. art, music, athletics, etc. but has difficulty in using these gifts, which could lead to frustrations, loss of self-respect, confidence, etc. which can in turn result in aggressive, hostile and antisocial behavior by the child.

According to a recent study by an interdisciplinary team of researchers at the University of Washington (1999), highlight that the dyslexic children use nearly five times the brain area as compared to the normal children while performing a simple language task. The study shows for the first time that there are chemical differences in the brain function of dyslexic and non-dyslexic children. Though, dyslexia is the most common learning difficulty, affecting an estimated 5 percent to 15 percent of children, dyslexic children have enormous talents in other parts of their brain and shine in many fields.

Identification of Reading Difficulties

In order to understand and identify reading difficulties, a thorough and formal assessment is usually conducted by a psychologist or an educationist. The testing tools mostly used are standardized tests other screening tools also. The whole assessment battery consists of tests, which gives an overall picture of the child's intellectual and academic achievements (Vito, 1991). Therefore the assessment for identifying the problems in reading requires tests for reading and intelligence level because the reading ability of the child should roughly match his/her intelligence level (Lewkowicz, 1996). But in order to identify the exact problem the child is encountering and to actually figure out the nature of the problem, the tests should be valid, reliable and practical. Otherwise the assessing procedure conducted, fails to trace out the real problem or difficulty, which the child has, and therefore gives a label to the child which is not his/her problem at all.

River (1999) raises a concern about the issue of assessing reading difficulties as his research findings give us a whole different perspective on reading disabilities. River questions the identification procedure to make the educators and other researchers think whether these people who are identified as having reading difficulties or dyslexia, are really disabled? He further explains that "may be the disability was in the method of teaching not the student!" (p.1). Leadbetter and Leadbetter (1993) also warns against the hasty identification of the students as having learning difficulties or reading difficulties based on their poor performance in the tests. They assert that this performance could be attributed to a variety of reasons like problems in art of the curriculum or some specific skills, some of which may be temporary, inappropriate teaching strategies, inadequate teaching methods, lack of language exposure, etc. It is also emphasized that not only is accurate identification necessary, but also the understanding of the reading difficulty itself is important for teachers to help the children overcome their learning challenges.

Some researchers had raised their concern in regard to using standardized tests, which can be questionable according to him, to all ages and levels of schooling, especially for primary children, as he explains that in these years, children's growth is uneven. Even testing students from backgrounds different from the culture in which the test was developed raises the probability of invalid tests (Brescia & Fortune, 1988). Similarly Schwarz (1995) is of the view that using standardized tests to identify learning difficulties presents problems. One of the problems highlighted by him is that the instruments designed to diagnose learning difficulties are usually normed on native English speakers and therefore the results cannot be reliably used with learners whose first language is not English. He further explains that portions of some of these tests can give a picture of the learners' strengths and weaknesses, but simple scores based on a whole test are not always reliable. According to Dockrell and McShane (1992):

> The task or tasks which a child has difficulty must be analyzed so that the component skills necessary for successful performance are understood. The child is the person currently experiencing difficulty with the task, so obviously it is important to have methods to assess the child's current cognitive abilities, together with any other relevant psychological abilities. Once these have been assessed, the cognitive demands that are made on the child's current abilities can be determined. The environment is the external context in which the child's difficulty is manifested; and aspects of the environment may be contributory factors to the child's learning difficulty. (p.8)

Therefore, it is recommended to develop one's own tests taking care of the students' level, language, cultural differences, etc (Brescia & Fortune, 1988). Antonoff (1998) also supports the diagnosis to be accurate and valid by emphasizing on the 'in depth, psycho educational testing' conducted by an expert 'to delineate any deficits or deviation' in the information processing, resulting in a diagnosis of learning difficulties. Thus formal 'psycho-linguistic assessment' is needed to assess reading difficulties or dyslexia, which has three major components; history gathering, interview with parents and the child, and testing of the child (Bright Solutions for Dyslexia, 1998). According to Beech (1985), the recent research work also suggests that:

> There are problems in making an accurate diagnosis for the selection of children for remedial reading. Furthermore, even in the remedial setting there seems to be little agreement amongst the experts as to what exactly an individual child's deficits are and what needs to be done in the future about the child. (p.38)

Sensenbaugh (1995) also supports the test validation by expressing the issue for educators, who are always looking for valid and reliable predictors of educational achievement. He explains that one of the reasons why the educators are so interested in phonemic awareness is that research indicates that it is the best predictor of early reading acquisition. It is even better than IQ, vocabulary, and listening comprehension. And therefore according to Smith (1992), it is important to remember that not all individuals who have problems with reading are dyslexic and it's diagnosis should only be done by a qualified reading professional.

Causes of Reading Difficulties

As mentioned earlier, many children with reading difficulties have deficiencies in their ability to process phonological information, which creates problems for them to relate letters of the alphabet to the sounds of language. For all the students, the processes of phonological awareness, including phonemic awareness, must be explicitly taught. Recent research seems to suggest that dyslexia stems from an underlying difficulty in phonological awareness (CLD, 1997; Turnbull, Turnbull, Shank, Leal, 1999). Children from culturally diverse backgrounds may have particular difficulties with phonological awareness. The language exposure at home, the reading exposure at an early age, and dialect all affect the ability of children to understand the phonological distinctions on which the English language is built. It is suggested that teachers must apply sensitive effort and use a variety of techniques to help children learn these skills when standard English is not spoken at home (Essential Learning Institute, 1995). However, Ramey (1998) refers to the University of Florida Brain Institute study, which highlights that, the "brain structure and hand preference may be as important as environment in influencing a child's ability to learn to read" (p.1). Lerner (1996) also emphasizes for the supportive environment for learning to read.

According to Smith's (1992) point of view, educators and researchers cannot agree on a specific and precise definition of dyslexia or its causes. He refers to Vellutino's (1987) research, which has challenged many commonly held beliefs about dyslexia and its causes and states that it "appears to be a complex linguistic deficiency marked by the inability to represent and access the sound of a word in order to help remember the word and the inability to break words into component sounds" (p.1). According to Pressley (1998), some primary grade students of normal or above-average intelligence, experience difficulty in learning to read. Moreover, these difficulties predict continuing reading difficulties throughout schooling. When the child experiences difficulties in learning to read, biological differences of children is often highlighted to be one of the major causes, which is explained to be the dis-functioning of the brain. Therefore, it makes it more difficult for the children with reading disabilities, even with intensive instruction that would be effective to most of the students. Thus the teaching of reading needs to be appropriate with well-structured reading approach that could facilitate the teaching of reading for children who are facing difficulties in learning to read.

The children having an average or above average IQ and are reading 1½ grades or more below grade level, may be dyslexic. True dyslexia affects about 3 to 6 % of the population, yet in some cases it is up to 50% of the students are not reading at grade level. But again it is very important to highlight that not all children reading below grade level are dyslexic. This means that the reason for most children not reading at grade level is ineffective reading instruction and therefore could be a cause of low reading performance. Reading difficulties can be a result of inappropriate teaching or faulty teaching that the child is exposed to (Larcombe, 1985; Smith, 1991; Dockrell & McShane, 1992). The inappropriate match of the learning tasks to the learner's ability levels or characteristics, make it worse for a learner who is trying to master tasks presented in the class (Larcombe, 1985). Usually, schools are not aware of these problems and therefore do not accommodate the individual differences, and hence increase the school's population of students experiencing learning difficulties (Smith, 1991). There may be a mismatch between the teaching styles of teachers and the learning styles of students (Larcombe, 1985; Leadbetter & Leadbetter, 1993, Schwarz, 1995; Reynolds, 1991). In order to have a close critical look at the situation, to see whether it is really the students' learning difficulties or is it the teachers' inadequate way of teaching, Smith (1991) cites Bateman (1974) who recommends that the terms like 'reading disability' should be substituted with 'teaching disability.' This means that the student is not the only one to be blamed, but the teaching is at times inappropriate and inadequate to meet the learning needs of individuals (Prumfrey & Delliot, 1993). But to differentiate between dyslexic children and children who fail to learn reading by poor instruction can be done by exposing the children to good and appropriate reading instructions. This would result in improving children's reading performance, who are not dyslexic but suffer due to poor teaching instructions. This would also help in identifying the dyslexic children who also suffer from having a specific learning disability (Child Development Institute, 1997).

Learning difficulties like dyslexia have been found to run within families (Lokerson, 1992b, Schwarz, 1995). Pressley (1998) states that, "when a child experiences difficulties in learning to read, a family history of reading problems, unaccompanied by evidence of a family history of low intelligence, may be one reason to suspect developmental dyslexia" (p.7). The hereditary factor, which seems to run in families, could be one of the causes for specific disorders in reading or dyslexia (Smith, 1992; Crowder & Wagner, 1992; Root, 1994; Bright Solutions of dyslexia, 1998). According to the research from Boston University and Emerson College, it is found that some of the children who had reading problems had nothing remarkable in their developmental histories except very low birth weight i.e. under 1500 grams. It was also speculated that the early medical difficulties may have an effect on language development that would not be apparent until the children start to learn to read (Menyuk, 1996). The children from poor backgrounds, limited proficiency in English, hearing impairments, preschool language impairments and children whose parents had difficulty learning to read are particularly at risk of arriving at school with weaknesses in these areas and hence falling behind at school. The majority of the reading problems faced by today's adolescents and adults are the result of the problems that might have been avoided or resolved in their early childhood years and steps should be taken to ensure that children overcome these obstacles during the primary grades (Snow, Burns & Griffin, 1998).

Thus, the major causes, which the literature indicates for children having reading difficulties are related, on one hand, to the hereditary factors, brain structure and its dis-functioning while, on the other hand, the child's background and environment, lack of language exposure, poor reading instructions and inappropriate teaching of reading could be responsible for his/her reading problems.

Dyslexia and Reading in a Second Language
According to Schwarz (1995) reading difficulties can also be due to a lack of previous educational experience, or ineffective study habits, or the interference of a learner's native language, which may complicate the process of learning a second language. Therefore the learners may show these difficulties in their second language only. He further states that, "in fact, some of the problems of learning disabled language learners may be similar to those of all students beginning to learn a second language, however, with the non-disabled learner, these problems should lessen over time" (p.2). According to Guron and Lundberg (2000), it is assumed that the reading skills of a normal reader will be more efficient and automatic when approaching a text in a native language (L1) than when faced with a text written in a second language (L2). Studies provide evidence that readers without specific learning difficulties gain access to the mental lexicon of L1 faster than that of L2 (Favreau, Komoda & Segalowitz, 1980; Segalowitz, 1986; Shimon & Sivan, 1994). Thus it seems that native language weaknesses inhibit the development of foreign language proficiency. Guron and Lundberg (2000) further explain that, "the dyslexic reader, who reads native language texts with poor efficiency and low automaticity is assumed to experience considerably less efficiency and lower automaticity when approaching an L2 text" (p.42). According to

Spolsky (1989) it is also evident that any physiology or biological limitations that block the learning of a first language will similarly block the learning of a second language. Regular symptoms of dyslexia such as phonological processing, poor working memory, poor auditory discrimination, confusion over syntax and faulty auditory sequencing are all expected to impair the development of L2 reading skills (Hoein & Lundberg, 1997; Crombie, 1997).

Remedial Strategies

As mentioned earlier, learning/reading difficulties are difficult to recognize at times as they are the 'hidden handicaps' (Lokerson, 1992a). Also, they exist on three levels i.e. mild, moderate and severe (William, 1990; Dockrell & McShane, 1992). Children with learning disabilities display a rather unique combination of problems in learning. Children, who fit into the regular school curriculum having mild learning difficulties, manage to overcome their learning disabilities with the help of occasional remedial teaching. Children who have a moderate difficulty level are those whose mastery level is slower and therefore need modifications in the curriculum offered to them with an extra help through a pull out program to cater for their individual learning needs. The children having severe learning difficulties need to learn and relearn many of the skills by drilling and reinforcement which could be done on a one to one basis to help them learn the coping strategies to facilitate their learning process (Kunc, 1992; Slavin, 1995; William, 1990).

Most reading difficulties which stem from factors such as poor instruction, lack of reading readiness, or cultural differences, which can be overcome with early intervention and intensive reading instruction. As Lerner (1996) highlights that, "intensive and systematic early intervention is needed for young children who are at-risk for reading failure" (p.1). Recent studies by Reid Lyon, the neuropsychologist at the National Institute Child Health and Human Development Department have shown that when students with severe reading problems are given early, intensive instruction, nearly 95% can reach the national average in reading ability. Pikulski (1997), the president of International Reading Association recommends that in order to make effective, early, extensive intervention programs must be both intensive and fast paced. Reading specialists should work with students individually or in very small groups (CEC Today, 1997). As Jackson and Roller (1993) also emphasize that, "reading failure ... can be prevented by the early identification of reading difficulties, followed by appropriate instruction" (p.1-2). Children have an easier time overcoming reading difficulties when problems are spotted early (Gupta & Coxhead, 1990). As Hornby (1997) explains, "children's language development precludes them from being able to use a phonetic alphabet unless the phonemes are specifically taught and phonemic awareness can be recovered at any age, but for children learning to read, the earlier the better" (p.188). Snow, Burns and Griffin (1998) also emphasize on early intervention to be having a positive impact on the child's learning process. Mostly research studies lay emphasis on early interventions to be the key to mend reading problems but that can be possible only when a well-structured reading program is implemented. Different reading programs are based on different reading approaches like whole language approach, basal approach, linguistic approach, phonetic approach and multi-sensory approach. These approaches are used in teaching of reading and range accordingly from the least structured to the well-structured reading approaches respectively. Some of the research studies suggest that there is no one way to teach reading and teachers need to be trained in teaching of reading. As Lerner (1996) emphasizes that "successful reading instructions requires a variety of approaches" (p.1).

Along with the effective implementation of the well-structured reading program, the teacher's positive attitude is also very important for the remediation purposes. The National Center for Learning Disabilities, the Orton Dyslexia Society and the Learning Disabilities Association of America (1996) give emphasis to the teachers as "an essential link between children with learning disabilities and the interventions" (p.1). As these institutions claim that there is no student with learning disability who cannot learn, if a teacher has received appropriate training and is willing to spend the time, using his or her expertise to teach with a 'positive attitude' to reach that child. Leadbetter and Leadbetter (1993) also put an emphasis on the positive attitude of the teacher towards helping students to cope up their learning difficulties. And they state that the "... teacher attitudes

27

play a powerful role in formulating a positive response to the challenge of meeting the needs of pupils with learning differences" (p.23). The literature on teachers' beliefs especially that on the attitude of dealing with the teacher's expectations from students, suggests that teachers' understandings in the area of special education needs has an important impact on teacher behaviour and attitude towards these students as well as their performance and achievement (Winebrenner, 1996). Cotterell (1980) also states:

> An understanding, sympathetic teacher is of vital importance to the child who is doing his utmost to succeed and making little progress. When taught in accordance with his needs a child with specific reading disability is able to learn and does not lack motivation. He tends to fail if left un-helped or taught in a group of mixed remedial problems. (p.10)

Research on teacher attitude towards children with learning difficulties has shown that teachers have 'low expectations' from these students (Hastings, Hewes, Lock & Witting, 1996). Lacey and Porter's (1996) survey of the teachers of pupils with learning difficulties and challenging behaviour, showed that teachers stated a need for training to work with this category of students. Smith (1992) highlights that many slow readers, who are not however dyslexic, can be helped with a variety of reading experiences to improve fluency. He states that, "a positive attitude on the part of the child is also crucial to the treatment of difficulties in reading and learning" (p.3). He further explains that teachers who have been working consistently with problem learners are very much aware of the role of the self in energizing learning, and the potential damage to the sense of self-worth that comes from the labeling. The child needs to feel loved and appreciated as an individual, whatever the level of difficulty is. Teachers and parents should appreciate children's thinking as the foundation of their language abilities and maintain some flexibility in their expectations regarding their children's development of decoding skills such as reading. For these children to feel successful, they need to become aware of their unique learning strengths, so that they may apply effectively while working to strengthen the lagging areas (Webb, 1992).

To summarize, the main reasons for reading difficulties are ineffective reading instructions, auditory perception difficulties, visual perception difficulties and language processing difficulties. It seems that reading problems will remain common in the children but successful early intervention programs strongly suggest that many of these problems are preventable.

Chapter Three
METHODOLOGY

Research Design

This research study is about children's reading difficulties in English and in order to answer the main research question, i.e. "How can teachers help children with reading difficulties in English at the primary level in a multi-lingual context of Pakistan?" a fieldwork of 8 weeks was conducted to identify:

➤ Different types of reading difficulties in children and their causes,

➤ Teachers' awareness to cater for children's reading difficulties,

➤ Different remedial strategies for dealing with children's reading difficulties,

➤ Possibilities and challenges faced by teachers in dealing with the children having reading difficulties.

Therefore, identifying children's reading difficulties in English as a second or a foreign language, comparing them across languages, investigating their relative causes to remediate the same, helping children in their learning process in a multi-lingual context like Pakistan, and highlighting the issues concerning identification and remediation of the reading difficulties gives the study its significance. As there has not been much research in our context on this topic, the study gives insights into related issues.

This research study consists of two major phases. The first phase comprised of analyzing the learners' difficulties in reading English at the primary level in one sample school. The second phase consisted of exploring the facilities available in remedial centres and other schools to cater for children's reading difficulties, in order to gain insights on how teachers can help children with reading difficulties in a multi-lingual context, similar to that of the sample school in phase I. The study used the following data collection sources:

➤ Untrained 'reading' teachers in the sample school,

➤ Standardized testing for identifying children's reading difficulties in the school,

➤ Reading specialist teachers in the remedial centres, &

> Trained reading teachers working in two 'elite' schools.

In the first phase, interviews and classroom observations of untrained reading teachers, who are teaching English language but are not trained as reading teachers to children at the primary level, were done to get an idea of whether these teachers were aware of reading difficulties in children or not. And if they were, what were they doing about it? Teachers teaching English, Urdu and Sindhi were interviewed to identify the children's reading difficulties across three languages. The findings also helped in comparing children's reading difficulties across languages. Standardized tests were also conducted with a randomly selected sample of class V children, to identify children with reading difficulties and the specific nature of these problems in reading in English. Thus the identification of reading difficulties of children was done both first by their teachers and through conducting Standardized tests.

The second phase of the study comprised of interviews and observations of remedial sessions conducted by the reading specialist teachers as well as trained reading teachers in remedial centres and identified private schools in Karachi which catered for the children's reading difficulties. The aim was to explore and understand, how they identify and cater for the children's reading difficulties. That helped me to derive future recommendations for the school context where the needs analysis was initially done. The suggestions would help to create awareness in the teachers in dealing with children with reading difficulties in their schools to help them in their learning process and possibly lead to a systematic approach to address this issue at the level of the school system, of which the sample is a part.

Setting and Research Location

The first phase of needs analysis was conducted in a private school in Karachi. The primary section of the school is run in double shift; the morning shift is for the girls and the afternoon shift for boys. Each section has 15 to 16 teachers and out of these teachers, 5 to 6 teachers teach English in their respective sections. There were 11 classes in each section. The average number of children in each class was approximately 40 to

45. Because of the contextual familiarity, as I had been teaching in the girls primary section for the last 10 years and had been experiencing children facing reading difficulties, I focused the research investigation in the primary girls section.

The second phase of the fieldwork was done in the following remedial centres in Karachi where children's reading difficulties are identified and catered for by the specialist professionals and trained teachers:

➤ Remedial Education for Assessment of Dyslexics (R.E.A.D),

➤ Centre for Assessment and Remedial Education (C.A.R.E),

➤ Institute for Behavioral Psychology (I.B.P), &

➤ Spell Bound (Centre for educational development).

In addition, the exploratory study in phase II included two private schools, where reading difficulties of the children are catered for by trained teachers in the respective field.

Research Sample

The main sample for this research study were untrained reading teachers from the sample school of the multi-lingual context, where children came from a middle class background. These teachers were interviewed and their reading lessons were observed, in order to identify their level of awareness towards children's reading difficulties and remedial strategies to cater for the same. In addition, a sample of the age group of children (girls) between 9 to 11 years of grade V was randomly selected for conducting some standardized tests to identify their reading difficulties. The sample of students selected was matched on the basis of age group, gender and educational level. The reading specialist teachers from the remedial centres and trained reading teachers from two identified private schools, working in association with these remedial centres, were also interviewed and their remedial reading sessions were observed.

Data Collection Procedure

The initial study focused on the identification of the level of teacher's awareness, children's reading difficulties and an intervention in one of the primary ESL classrooms. It was planned to introduce remedial strategies in the classroom with the help of the teacher, in order to help children overcome their reading difficulties. This would be done after conducting the Standardized reading tests, to identify children's reading difficulties. It was hoped that the possibilities, which exist and challenges encountered by teachers in dealing with children's reading difficulties in the classrooms would be highlighted during this process and recorded. The aim was to focus on two or three students, identified as having reading difficulties, throughout the study to keep a track of their progress and performance. It was planned to be a whole class intervention rather than a pull out program. However, it was soon realized that it would not be possible to follow this proposed plan as both the conducting of tests to identify children's reading difficulties and implementing the remedial strategies needed specialist knowledge and prior training. Hence, the study was refocused at an early stage. Thus instead of intervention, it was decided to look at how reading difficulties were catered for by some remedial centres in the city, as well as schools working in association with these centres. The design of the final study fieldwork is as below:

Phase I

Negotiating entry

I managed to negotiate entry into the sample school by discussing the research topic 'Reading difficulties in children' and the time frame for 8 weeks of my fieldwork, with the principal of the school. She was given an official letter from the academic director of IED, which certified me as a student of the M.Ed. program and also a researcher for this study.

Interviewing the teachers

The principal gave me the teachers' timetable to identify teachers and to negotiate with them about the interview schedule. She also put up a notice in the staff room, introducing me, my research topic and asking the teachers to co-operate with me in my study. As it was my school, which had sponsored me for the M.Ed. program, it hardly took me an hour to negotiate and schedule interviews with the teachers. I managed to interview altogether 11 teachers by using a semi-structured interview. Out of which, 9 teachers were teaching English and 2 were teaching Urdu and Sindhi languages at the primary level. This was done to see the awareness level of their children's reading difficulties and to get some information which would help in identifying the types of reading difficulties faced by children and also to determine whether these are the same or different, across languages.

Class observations

Out of the nine English teachers interviewed, seven were teachers of classes I to III, teaching the Integrated Primary Curriculum (IPC). Apart from teaching English, these teachers were teaching Mathematics, Science and Social Studies also. The remaining two teachers were teaching classes IV and V. These two teachers were observed in their reading classes. On the one hand, these observations gave an idea of the children's reading level and the reading problems they were encountering, whereas on the other hand, they gave an authenticity to the data collected from the teachers' interviews to find out how were they teaching reading and helping the children with their reading problems.

Assessment of children's reading difficulties with Standardized tests

The Standardized screening tests for assessing children's reading difficulties were used for the identification of children's reading difficulties. Since the research study focused on identifying the children's oral reading difficulties, the tests selected were Standard Progressive Matrices (SPM), Wide Range Achievement Test- Revised (WRAT-R) and Slosson Oral Reading Test (SORT). These tests are standardized on the native English population. The justification for selecting them for this context was the non-availability of other local tests. Also the clinics and the remedial centres in our context are using the same tests for diagnosing children's reading difficulties. As the tests have copyrights and need specialized training, I had to seek help from a clinical psychologist at AKU-SON, who is currently working on her doctorate in reading difficulties. She was also given an official letter from IED, which certified me as a researcher for this study. These tests were level 1 tests, which fitted to the age group of grade V student's i.e. from 9 to 11 years. The identified grade V class for conducting these tests had 43 students. The tests were scheduled for three to four weeks from 9:00 a.m. to 12:00 noon. The sample class was randomly divided into two groups to facilitate the testing procedure planned.

34

But because the testing procedure was time consuming, it was only possible to assess one group consisting of 21 students in the given time period.

These tests were negotiated, planned and scheduled with the permission of the school's principal and the parents of grade V children in the school. The teachers and students of the class, in which the testing was being conducted, were informed. The principal also informed the parents about the tests by sending a letter mentioning the purpose and rationale for conducting these tests for getting their consent. And test results were only to be used for diagnostic purposes in the study, they were kept confidential. I also asked the resource person for a consent letter, mentioning that the test results would be kept confidential and could be used for other research purposes only with prior permission of the school and other concerned stakeholders. A copy of this letter was given to the school's principal, to assure the confidentiality of test results. A brief description of the tests is given below which were conducted for the identifying reading difficulties in children:

Standard Progressive Matrices (SPM)

It gives an account of the cognitive profile of the children. This test was taken in a group of 21 students and which took approximately 45 to 55 minutes. The test comprised a number of designs in which a piece of the design was missing. There were a number of choices down the design for the children to choose for the correct piece, which fitted the actual design. The children were asked to write the correct answer number in the answer sheet. The designs got more complicated and difficult as the child proceeded with the test. The child had to be very attentive in order to concentrate on the different angles of the design to get a correct answer.

Wide Range Achievement Test-Revised (WRAT-R)

It consists of three components i.e. reading, writing (spelling) and arithmetic - the 3R s of the test. Only the reading and spelling parts of the test were done, as the arithmetic part was not relevant to this research study. The reading component comprised of a list of words, which the students had to read, and after 10 consecutive errors, the child was asked to stop reading. The list of words was organized in such a way that they became difficult as one proceeded reading them. This test was done on an individual basis and it took at least 10 minutes per child. The writing component also comprised a list of words that were organized from easy to difficult. This was done in order to understand more prominently the types of reading errors, as they are more highlighted and pronounced in the written work of the children. These words were dictated to children in-groups of 20 as a spelling test. The students were given answer sheets to write on. As it was a long list of 45 words, the test took 20 to 25 minutes per group. Both the components helped in the identification of the types of errors children made in oral reading and pronunciation, which helped in tapping the reading difficulties of children.

Slosson Oral Reading Test (SORT)

It consisted of a graded list of words according to different grade level of the children. The child was asked to start reading from a level below their actual grade levels and the teacher noted the errors. On one hand, if the child had difficulties in reading that list, the teacher asked the child to continue reading one more grade below, till the child was able to read one complete graded list without any errors. If on the other hand, if the child was able to read that list, then the teacher asked the child to read the list next accordingly and continued till the child was able to read. This test was taken individually and it took approximately 10 minutes per child.

As mentioned before, it was realized very early that the conducting of the tests needs specialized training and cannot be done by the researcher alone. Thus, the tests took a much longer time then planned due to prior commitments of the resource person. Therefore, while the testing process continued in the school, I started my visits to remedial centres and other identified schools to explore facilities and resources for identifying children's reading difficulties and remediating the same in these institutions.

Phase II
Visits to remedial centres and other schools
I visited four remedial centres in Karachi whereby I got to interview reading

36

specialist teachers who are professionally involved in catering for children's reading difficulties. I also observed their remedial reading sessions. In addition, using a semi-structured interview, I interviewed two trained reading teachers from selected schools, working in association with these centres. I also wanted to visit the five schools, identified by the remedial centres as catering for children's reading difficulties. These schools can be described as 'high-income' schools or schools for the 'elite' class children. But as it was the end of their academic year, these schools were also conducting their final exams. So it was not possible for me to conduct any research in those schools. However, the teacher of one of these schools allowed me to observe a lesson planned for her remedial training in her school especially arranged for this purpose.

Data Analysis Procedure

The data for this research study were collected through conducting interviews of trained and untrained teachers, observing their reading lessons and conducting standardized tests for assessing children's reading difficulties in one school. Semi-structured interview schedules were used to interview teachers. For remedial sessions, observation field notes were taken. These interviews and observations were audio recorded, which helped in transcribing. No doubt, transcribing the interviews took a lot of time, but it also gave a chance of understanding and analyzing the data in the process. The transcribed interviews and observation field notes were read several times, in order to become more familiar with the data. Then the main findings from the data were highlighted and coded according to the emerging themes and issues, which helped in answering the research questions. Moreover, the standardized reading tests were marked, the test scores analyzed and the results interpreted for the identification of reading difficulties of children in the sample school, where English is the second or third language of the children.

Limitations of the Study

The limitations of the study are as follows:

➤ Since the reading tests were conducted in one primary school with a limited sample of 21 children, the findings cannot be generalized to all primary school children in

37

Pakistan.

➢ Interviews and remedial observations were not possible in the five identified schools where children's reading difficulties are catered for, because of the final exams at the end of the academic year.

➢ Because of the non-availability of the local tests to identify children's reading difficulties, the Standardized tests developed for a different native population of U.S.A were used; therefore the results had to be interpreted with caution.

Ethical Issues

The following ethical issues were taken care of:

➢ Participation of the teachers in the study depended on their willingness and interest.

➢ Consent of the school management and the parents of grade V children was taken for conducting the tests to identify children's reading difficulties.

➢ Confidentiality of the children identified as having reading difficulties, to avoid labeling and misuse of this information.

➢ Consent of the remedial centres and trained teachers was taken for observing remedial teaching sessions.

Generalizability of the Study

As the tests were conducted to identify reading difficulties of children in one of the 'middle-class' multi-lingual schools, the findings cannot be generalized to all the schools. To a certain extent, it has a limited generalizability to similar school contexts of Karachi, where the students come from middle class backgrounds, where English is their second or third language and where English is the medium of instruction. Thus, the findings might not be generalized to other elite schools, where the students come from a high socio-economic background and where English is spoken almost as their native language. Similarly, the findings related to the remedial centres and these elite schools that are catering for the children's reading difficulties shows limited generalizability. However, the kinds of reading difficulties identified by the teachers of these elite schools and remedial centres, match to some extent, the errors identified by the tests in the sample school.

Chapter Four

FINDINGS AND DISCUSSION

The chapter presents the analysis and discussion of the research study findings on reading difficulties in children. As mentioned earlier, this research study was conducted on the assumptions that children do have different kinds of reading difficulties. However, most of the teachers are not aware of these reading difficulties and are therefore not catering for the same. Even if teachers are aware, they are not trained enough to assess children's reading difficulties, and to implement specific remedial reading strategies in order to help children to overcome the reading difficulties in the classrooms. Also, throughout the research study, reading difficulties refer to children's oral reading difficulties in English language.

As discussed in the methodology chapter, the study was divided into two phases. The first phase focused on finding out the awareness level of the teachers with regard to children's reading difficulties in English language. For this, interviews were conducted with language teachers and their reading lessons were observed. Standardized tests were also conducted with a randomly selected sample of twenty-one students of class V, to identify their reading difficulties. The second phase explored the facilities and resources available in different remedial centres and other schools for dealing with children's reading difficulties. The analysis and findings of both the phases are presented below:

Identifying Children's Reading Difficulties

The interviews of untrained reading teachers in the sample school revealed that they were unaware of the specific reading difficulties in children but they identified some common reading problems faced by the children, which they had experienced in their classrooms. According to the teachers, children faced reading problems related to the mechanics of reading e.g. problems like pronunciation, word recognition and unfamiliar vocabulary. The teachers mentioned that along with these problems, students have understanding and comprehension problems as well. All the language teachers, either of

English, Urdu or Sindhi, highlighted these reading problems, but had no idea of more specific reading difficulties. This is evident in one of the teachers' interview:

> I don't know exactly what the reading difficulties in children are but I know that they have reading problems such as pronunciation problems, comprehension problems, etc. and as we teachers discuss, these problems are not only in English language but also are there in the Urdu and Sindhi classes. (IUTA)

Another teacher in the interview expressed that, "children face pronunciation and comprehension problems and should know the sounds of the letters in order to read properly" (IUT1). These perceptions of the teachers were confirmed during the observation of reading lessons. In contrast, the specialist and trained teachers' not only observed that children do have reading difficulties but they also highlighted specific reading difficulties such as reversals, omissions, substitutions, deletions, repetitions and comprehension problems. One of the trained teachers highlighted that:

> The children who have reading difficulties do not understand what they are reading. And they just do sight-reading. Some children cannot even do sight-reading. For e.g. this child whom I was teaching cannot do sight-reading. All the time he confuses t and b. I have to tell him that the b-ball comes first and t-bat comes after. So I tell him to put the thumb like this and see it. Every time he has to connect something with it. Sometimes he knows it but there is still confusion in that. Like saw and was. Sometimes he reads 'saw' as 'was' and … like 'spot,' did you notice he was reading s-o-p-t. Then I said, sound it out and then read it. This child has got reading problems. (ITT1)

Reading difficulties identified by specialists and trained reading teachers have also been highlighted in literature on reading difficulties (Shaywitz, 1996a; Bryant & Bradley, 1985). However, in literature, these reading difficulties are more or less divided into two major areas of decoding and comprehension (CLD, 1997; Turnbull, Shank, Leal, 1999; Lokerson, 1992a; Pollock & Waller, 1997). Furthermore, the researchers explain that the decoding difficulties sometimes result in comprehension difficulties. In addition the nature of these reading difficulties could be mild, moderate or severe (Dockrell & McShane, 1992; William, 1990).

Assessing Children's Reading Difficulties through Standardized Tests

To identify the child's reading difficulties; standardized tests and other screening tools are used by remedial centers. This was explained by one reading specialist teacher as follows:

> We get a lot of children who do lot of substitutes, one word for the other. We have tests that we carry out. We do GORT. This is the oral reading test. This gives you all the errors; substitutions, deleting of words, if you have a visual problem then you substitute whole words because you are reading in context, like for alligator you say crocodile. Then there is missing out words while reading, repetition of words, etc. (IST1)

One of the trained teachers highlighted that even though they were trained as reading teachers, they were unable to assess the children, as this needed further specialized training. It seems that the training provided by remedial centres does not equip the reading teachers with adequate skills and knowledge for using the psycho-educational assessment tools to identify children's reading difficulties. These specialized trainings equips teachers with skills to assess and diagnose the children's reading difficulties, but again an academic educationist in this special field is needed to develop and plan for catering to individual needs of these children. Thus, the remedial strategies differ according to the specific needs of the children facing reading difficulties.

It was found that the available Standardized tests, which have been developed for the native speakers of English, seem to be inappropriate for the identification of children's reading difficulties, who belong to a background where they did not have much exposure to English language as they learnt it as a second, third or foreign language. One of the reading specialist teachers expressed that:

41

All these tests are standardized on the American population. It is okay for us because the schools we are dealing are elite schools, which use foreign books. So kids are aware of that kind of culture and it is not a new world for them. (IST2)

Another trained teachers also emphasized the same issue by saying that:

These tests are very intensive. But basically our problem is that usually children are not good in English and they are all English based. I think they should be in Urdu or translated. That is very important. Naturally they are for those children whose language is English, but our language is not English. And definitely an intelligent child also who is not good in English will not be able to do those tests. And we will label him that he is not intelligent and has a learning problem. (ITT1)

Reading difficulties of children are usually assessed in oral reading and comprehension skills. As mentioned earlier, Standardized oral reading tests were used in the present study to identify the reading difficulties of a random sample of 21 students in grade V in the sample school. These tests were the Slosson Oral Reading Test (SORT) and Wide Range Achievement Test - Revised (WRAT-R). These tests were selected side by side to give authenticity to the test results for oral reading. With this the Standard Progressive Matrices (SPM), a cognitive profile test was also conducted to have an idea of the IQ level. This helped in correlating children's reading age and reading level as has been suggested by the literature that the correlation between the children's reading skills and IQ level, so as to understand the child's cognitive level (Frost & Emery, 1995; Lewkowicz, 1996). As these tests were standardized on the English native population, the justification for selecting them for our context was the non-availability of other local tests. Also these tests are being used in our context for the diagnostic and research purposes in clinics and also for remedial teaching in the remedial centres. Instructions for the tests were given both in English and Urdu to enable students to understand the tasks in the tests.

The results of the tests are given below:

TABLE 1

Standardized Test Results

S.#.	Age	Spm	Wratrr1	Wratrr2	Wratrs1	Wratrs2	Sort	Sch-A
1	9.7	76	*71	2B	79	2M	2.2	73.1
2	9.9	81	*71	2B	79	2M	4.4	75.6
3	9.8	81	*70	2B	67	1E	3.0	80.0
4	9.1	100	77	2M	96	3E	3.8	42.5
5	9.7	76	107	5B	106	5B	5.2	56.2
6	9.8	100	109	5E	54	1M	7.4	57.5
7	9.7	76	67	2B	72	2B	3.2	31.2
8	9.3	76	96	3E	90	3B	5.6	56.8
9	10	76	92	3E	80	2E	5.7	71.2
10	9.9	110	117	7B	107	5B	8.0	78.7
11	9.4	94	91	3B	95	3E	5.3	81.2
12	9.7	120	128	8A	125	7E	8.5	82.5
13	9.7	76	115	8E	111	8A	7.3	85.0
14	9.8	76	97	3E	101	4E	6.6	57.5
15	9.1	100	*70	2B	86	2E	4.3	41.8
16	8.11	76	108	4E	107	4E	7.9	86.2
17	9.1	90	101	4E	99	4B	8.0	53.1
18	9.11	76	110	5E	101	4E	8.0	88.7
19	9.8	87	111	2B	72	2B	3.1	60.0
20	9.6	100	83	2E	84	2E	3.5	72.5
21	9.7	81	*65	1E	74	2B	2.6	38.1

Key:

Spm = Standard Progressive Matrices (IQ) result

Wratrr1= Wide Range Achievement Range- Revised (Standard score for reading)

Wratrr2= Wide Range Achievement Range- Revised (Grade equivalent for reading)

Wratrs1 = Wide Range Achievement Range- Revised (Standard score for spelling)

Wratrs2 = Wide Range Achievement Range- Revised (Grade equivalent for spelling)

Sort = Slosson Oral Reading Test (reading level)

Sch-A = School Achievement (Overall performance for the month of May)

2B = Beginning of grade 2

2M = Middle of grade 2

2E = End of grade 2

8A = Above grade 8

2.2 = 2 grade level + 2 months

Analysis of the Test Results

The criteria for identifying students with reading difficulties was one standard deviation below the standard mean of WRAT-R reading test scores, that would be in this case, less than 74 (standard mean) score of reading. This means that the children in grade 5 should at least have a reading level of grade 3, i.e. those children whose scores were two reading grades below the grade level 5.1, (which means grade level 5 + 1 month of class V learning exposure as these tests were conducted in the month of May and the new academic year starts from April) which the child was at the time of testing, are 'reading disabled.' Literature suggests that the children with an average IQ and reading one and a half grades or more below grade level, may be labeled as 'reading disabled' (Hornsby, 1984). Using the above criteria, 6 children (No. 1, 2, 3, 7, 15 & 21) were identified (See table 1) as 'potential cases' or 'risk cases' of dyslexia i.e. children with average or above average IQ but their reading level not in accordance to their IQ level. For e.g. if the child's IQ is 90, that means he/she is 10 points behind the average IQ level. As 10 points of IQ level is equal to 1 year of reading age, therefore the child of grade V level, having an IQ of 90, means that this child should have a reading age of grade 4 level. Again it would have been much more helpful to understand the reading level of students as compared to the scores of the school achievement in reading, but since the school does not have separate reading tests, therefore the overall performance of the students for the month of May was used to get an idea of the level of performance of the child in school tests. It was interesting to note that the three children out of the sample of 21, which the teacher identified as having severe reading problems, were also in the list of six students who were diagnosed by the tests as having severe reading difficulties.

TABLE 2

Showing a comparison of the two reading tests results

S.#.	AGE	SPM	Wratrr1	WRAT-R	SORT	School
		IQ	Reading Score	Reading Level	Reading Level	Academic Performance
1*	9.7	76	*71	2B*	2.2*	73.1
2*	9.9	81	*71	2B*	4.4*	75.6
3*	9.8	81	*70	2B*	3.0*	80.0
4	9.1	100	77	2M*	3.8	42.5
5	9.7	76	107	5B	5.2	56.2
6	9.8	100	109	5E	7.4	57.5
7*	9.7	76	67	2B*	3.2*	31.2*
8	9.3	76	96	3E	5.6	56.8
9	10	76	92	3E	5.7	71.2
10	9.9	110	117	7B	8.0	78.7
11	9.4	94	91	3B	5.3	81.2
12	9.7	120	128	8A	8.5	82.5
13	9.7	76	115	8E	7.3	85.0
14	9.8	76	97	3E	6.6	57.5
15*	9.1	100	*70	2B*	4.3*	41.8*
16	8.11	76	108	4E	7.9	86.2
17	9.1	90	101	4E	8.0	53.1
18	9.11	76	110	5E	8.0	88.7
19	9.8	87	111	2B*	3.1	60.0
20	9.6	100	83	2E*	3.5	72.5
21*	9.7	81	*65	1E*	2.6*	38.1*

* The children identified with severe reading difficulties by the Standardized reading tests.

As mentioned earlier, two different types of reading tests were given to check students' reading errors. In addition, the spelling test was given to understand and identify errors more prominently. The tests' results were correlated to determine the accuracy of results. There were only 3 children (No. 7, 15 & 21) out of the sample of 21 children, whose scores were comparable on the two reading tests conducted i.e. WRAT-R and SORT. (See table 2). In fact, when the two reading test results were compared, the SORT results showed much higher reading grades as compared to the WRAT-R's reading level (See table 2). According to WRAT-R scores, out of 21 students, 9 were shown as reading disabled (No. 1, 2, 3, 4, 7, 15, 19, 20 & 21) while only 3 students (No. 1, 3 & 21) were as reading disabled by the SORT scores. This shows that test one's score identified the child as 'reading disabled,' however this was not confirmed by the same child's score on the other test. Therefore the validity of these tests scores needs to be questioned.

The reasons for this difference in test results could be that the word list in the WRAT-R test became more difficult as it proceeded as compared to the SORT word list. Moreover, the words present in the test list were not contextually relevant since the vocabulary used in the tests reflects the curriculum and textbooks, which are graded according to the native speakers of English. It was also observed, when the children were asked to read out the words from the reading list, that they found the WRAT-R vocabulary level to be more difficult than the SORT graded list of words. Though there was little correlation in the reading tests' scores of the sample children. This was not considered a major problem in the study as the main objective for conducting these tests was to identify the types of reading errors made by the children and not the number of errors committed by the children with reading difficulties.

The findings from the standardized tests conducted to identify the children's oral reading difficulties, highlighted both visual perceptual errors and auditory perceptual errors. This was prominent in the reading as well as spelling components of the tests conducted as there were problems identified between children's sight and phonetic words. It was analyzed that by sound, the words seemed to have been pronounced correctly by the children, but by sight they were incorrect (for e.g. 'brief' was spelled as 'breef,' 'watch' was spelled as 'wach,' 'criticize' was spelled as 'critisize,' 'familiar' was spelled as 'femiliyar,' 'dress' was spelled as 'drace,' 'explain' was spelled as 'explane,'etc). The kind of reading errors the children made were of *inclusions* and *omissions* (for e.g. 'marriage' was read as 'marry,' 'lame' was read as 'lamp,' 'lip' was read as 'lap,' 'plot' was read as 'pot,' 'felt' was read as 'feet,' etc), *distortions* (for e.g. 'reward' was read as 'river,' 'claimed' was read as 'climate,' 'tray' was read as 'try,' 'approve' was read as 'awake,' 'huge' was read as 'hungry,' etc), *reversals* (for e.g. 'bulk' was read as 'pluk,' or 'bluk,' 'pot' was read as 'top,' 'shell' was read as 'spell,'etc), and *substitutions* (for e.g. 'speechless' was read as 'shapeless,' 'threshold' was read as 'treehold,' etc). These errors were mostly phonetically correct but showed difficulties with sight words.

The reasons for the reading errors identified could be the lack of language exposure as English is not the native language of the sample population, while these tests are developed for the native speakers. Testing students from different backgrounds and cultures in which the test was not developed, raises the probability of invalid tests. Consequently a number of researchers laid a great deal of emphasis on accurate diagnosis (Brescia & Fortune, 1988; Schwarz, 1995; Beech, 1985; Smith, 1992; Sensenbaugh, 1995). Another reason for children's errors in reading could be due to the teaching of reading in the school particularly the teacher's pronunciation for e.g. 'imply' was read as 'implee,' 'clarify' was read as 'clarifee,' by most of the children. Also while analyzing the reading errors of these children, it was observed that the number of reading errors were more prominent in the reading tests as compared to the spelling test. However, when analyzed, these errors were more prominent in the spelling test than in the reading tests. But this evidence is not enough to label these children as 'reading disabled' because the test validity is at question as these tests are developed on a population whose native language is English, unlike the sample population comprised of children for whom English is a second or third or a foreign language. And also their proficiency level cannot be compared to the native speakers as they might not be exposed to the kind of vocabulary present in the reading tests' lists. In addition, few research studies also warn against the hasty identification of the students and labeling them as 'reading disabled' based on their poor performance in the tests (Leadbetter & Leadbetter, 1993; River, 1999).

Reading Difficulties vs. Language Difficulties

It was discovered that some children have language problems, some have reading difficulties and some have both. While interviewing the teachers, one of the issues raised by them, was referred to assessing and identifying reading difficulties, and more importantly, the problems in distinguishing between reading difficulties and language difficulties. One of the reading teachers explained that:

> Language is a problem because we are not teaching English language from
> the beginning. They speak in Urdu all the time. The thing is that when the
> child is writing opposite like all the words, then there is something, extra
> ordinary. (ITT1)

Literature also highlights the issue of distinguishing between reading difficulties and language problems. The teacher highlighted children's mistakes and errors in reading such as reversals, omissions, substitutions, etc. of letters and words. These reading problems stand out to be very extra ordinary and odd in comparison to the overall performances of other children in their classrooms. One of the specialist reading teachers highlighted the problem of conducting remedial teaching with children who are not proficient in English as follows:

> Now is it an ESL concern or a learning disability? I think being in the
> school, I think you can do it. So you see both can be dealt. But if it is a
> major ESL, then it is very difficult for us to teach. And it is difficult
> because it is all different fields. My program is conceptual based, we
> actually teach the kid a different lingual, we teach them concepts, and you
> can't really teach ... you can't really translate these concepts in Urdu.
> (IST2)

48

However, the remedial centres have started a separate program for children with low language proficiency in English. As one of the specialist teachers from the remedial centre said that:

> And what we are doing now is that we are introducing an ESL program because that's a big problem, English as a second language. Sometimes because of this problem a child shows learning disability but actually it is not. And we know now with our experience that a child who can not read and write or who can not understand the language. Can you imagine a child who have never spoken English, he speaks Urdu or Sindhi or any other language in the house and suddenly you put this child in such a class where English is throughout spoken ....Then it comes out as if the child has got learning disability but it is because he just can not understand the language. (IST1)

Causes Identified for Reading Difficulties

One of the major reasons identified by the teachers for children having reading problems in the multi-lingual context of Pakistan is home environment, where the children do not speak English, as it is not their first language. It was also mentioned that some of the students have reading problems because they have lack of vocabulary in the language, which hinders them in reading. Thus it was felt that children, who are exposed to an environment at home where English is spoken, are also good readers. This is highlighted in one of the responses given by the teachers, "the major problem is at home. Students do not speak in English. Their mother tongue is Urdu or other language. Some children speak English at home and are also good readers in the class" (IUT3).

Another teacher raised the concern of not having reading assessment in the exams by commenting that:

> Parents also are not interested in their children's reading, rather they ask about their children's written work and progress because exams are only written oriented and there is no reading assessment. You see, if children have reading problems, they also have problems in writing. (IUT7)

The teachers however, felt that reading should be given importance. It was suggested by one of the teachers that, "parental involvement helps children to read as it also helps in building children's confidence and therefore helps in the children who feel hesitation in reading in front of the class." (IUTA)

The teachers in the sample school mentioned that some of the English teachers do not speak in English with their students in the classrooms. This was also one of the reasons highlighted by the teachers for students not taking interest in reading and their hesitation in speaking English because of the lack of English language exposure, both in schools and at homes. But it was observed that in all the reading lessons the teachers spoke in English throughout the class period. It could be due to my presence in the classroom as an observer, as the students seemed to be unable to respond well in English. Therefore it can be concluded that it was not a usual practice. Both the teachers and reading specialists' highlighted that the teaching of reading in schools seems to be inappropriate. One of the trained reading teachers commented:

> I have noticed that language skills like reading and writing are not taught as a process but it is taught as a product. The child has to recall and reproduce in the exams and therefore teachers teach according to the exams, so language skills are not taught in an appropriate way and may be therefore these problems arise. Of course there are neurological causes for learning disabilities. It is the dis-functioning of the brain, which create some of these problems. (ITT2)

It came out very clearly in the teachers' interviews that reading is not taught properly in the previous classes. As one of the teachers mentioned that, "base is not strong for teaching of reading at the initial stage, it is weak. Pre-primary teachings should give more time to reading and teaching matching of sounds and letters effectively" (IUT4). One of the teachers in the interview expressed that, "children face difficulties in reading when they come from kindergarten, they cannot read and pronounce words" (IUT2). The teacher of the present class is found to be blaming the previous class teacher for not teaching reading properly. The interviews also revealed the issue that there was lack of co-ordination between the teachers and the planning for teaching of reading systematically. Some of the teachers also shared that they have some students in their classrooms, who are very slow readers probably due to problems in reading. One of the teachers in the school seemed to have some awareness about the children's learning difficulties as she had attended a summer workshop on the same topic. However, she was unable to identify specific reading problems in children and cater for the same. She explained that the workshop had not prepared her specifically for identifying reading problems or provided her with strategies for dealing with them.

To summarize, reading difficulties in children whose first language is not English could be attributed to one or more of the following reasons:

- Lack of conducive learning environment in the classroom,
- Lack of parental involvement in developing children's reading skills,
- Bi-lingual or multi-lingual context with no English language exposure,
- Not enough emphasis on developing reading skills in the school as they are not a part of children's academic examinations, and
- Inappropriate instructional methods for teaching reading.

As discussed above, the untrained reading teachers were not able to identify specific causes for the reading problems. However, the reading specialist teachers were in a position to identify specific reasons for reading difficulties as they were trained and had specialized skills for using sophisticated testing tools to assess children's reading difficulties. These causes identified by the reading teachers are also supported by the literature (Essential Learning Institute, 1995; Child Development Institute, 1997, Antonoff, 1998; Larcombe, 1985; Dockrell & McShane, 1992; River, 1999; Leadbetter & Leadbetter, 1993; Jackson & Roller, 1993). In addition, the dis-functioning of the brain has been identified as one of the major causes of reading difficulties (Ramey, 1998; Pressley, 1998). Some research studies suggest that reading difficulties are also due to underlying problems in phonological awareness and complex linguistic deficiency (CLD, 1997; Turnbull, Turnbull, Shank, Leal, 1999; Vellutino, 1987), whereas others highlight hereditary factor to be the main cause (Pressley, 1998; Lokerson, 1992b, Schwarz, 1995;

Smith, 1992; Crowder & Wagner, 1992; Root, 1994; Bright Solutions of dyslexia, 1998). Literature studies also highlight developmental histories like children's early medical difficulties and their low birth weight to be the causes of reading difficulties (Menyuk, 1996). However, none of these causes were identified in the study.

Do Teachers Cater for Children's Reading Difficulties?

Every teacher interviewed expressed that reading is very important in the learning process of the children as well as adults and therefore should be taught properly in the classrooms. All the teachers expressed in their interviews that reading is the base of learning as it gives the children a lot of knowledge when they read books. The most common way for teaching reading in the classrooms was observed to be reading aloud, drilling and silent reading. The teachers of lower classes mentioned that they usually read the text aloud, ask the students to repeat, write the difficult words on the black board for pronunciation and meaning, and then ask the students to read aloud or sometimes read silently. Sometimes peer or group reading is also done in the classroom.

The most common tasks after reading the text are comprehension exercises to checking students' understanding. The teachers mentioned that they also explain the text, if it is not understood by the students. At times some of the teachers used pictures, story telling, drama, newspapers, storybooks, role-play and cartoons to create interest and motivation. The teachers added that flash cards are also used for vocabulary enhancement and for improving spellings, which would in turn help in both reading and writing. The reading observations also confirmed that the teachers give more emphasis on students' comprehension skills, rather than teaching oral reading skills.

Thus it seems that decoding skills for e.g. the matching of the sounds with letters and the combination of the words are not taught to the students. One of the teachers expressed that, "to teach reading, teachers should be trained to help the children teach and overcome their reading problems" (IUT3). Another teacher commented that:

The students should know the sounds of the letters and pronunciation, sounds forming small lettered words and syllables, etc. These are some of

52

the basic skills, which should be taught to the children. Phonics and joining of letters and sounds will help children to read and write as they could spell out the words. (IUT5)

One of the teachers also mentioned that:

Silent reading is not the correct way of teaching reading to the students [at the primary level]. As English is not our first language, students have problems in pronouncing and understanding the words and text, so reading silently does not help students to read and understand the text which they don't know. (IUT8)

It was observed that there are different types of reading programs implemented in the sample school, such as Oxford Reading Tree (ORT), Ginn Reading Program, Silent & Home Reading Programs. In addition, Ginn reading books are used in the silent reading periods, which are twice a week i.e. on Tuesday & Thursday for 20 minutes in the morning. However, as one of the teachers said, "Reading periods are very short; therefore individual attention cannot be given to the students. We have to teach the topics, grammar, as well as do the corrections. No time for helping students in their reading problems" (IUT1). The solution to this problem was shared by a teacher who said that, "I usually make groups of children, then I can put more attention to the slow readers' groups or the groups having other reading problems" (IUT4). It seems that the Ginn reading books and the textbooks are the reading materials used for reading in the classrooms. It was evident in all the classroom observations of reading lessons that the teachers spoke in English in the class. It was highlighted in the teachers' interview that while the students read silently, the teacher went round the class and monitored by helping them in their reading process. This was also observed to be the case in the reading lesson. It was observed in one of the class that when the students reading silently, the teacher also read silently (CO4). This reflects that the teacher wanted to create an environment for reading in the classroom. One of the teachers also suggested that:

Reading of the stories collected from the newspapers by the students could be brought in the class and then they can exchange and read. The same can be done for storybooks and other books. This can help to create reading environment in the classroom. (IUTB)

It was also observed that the teacher tried to help the students to pronounce the difficult words by breaking the syllables and was observed helping the students to read out the words by themselves in the reading lessons. The teacher also wrote some of the difficult words on the black board and helped the whole class to pronounce them. For e.g. the teacher wrote the difficult words on the board like coyote, lay, pronghorn, still, led, etc. and explained the meanings of these words through pictures and asking probing questions as well as helped the students in pronouncing (CO3). It was also observed that for making the students understand the text, the teacher asked questions and also explained if the students did not understand the text read in the reading lessons. Moreover, the teacher sometimes wrote the instructions on the board for students to read and follow. For e.g. the teacher wrote, "Take out your pupil's book. Read Unit 2 for reading 10 minutes (pg. 6 & 7). Then I'll ask you questions and today we will do W.B exercise" (CO3).

It was found that there were library periods and also specific reading periods in the class timetable, which were allocated specially for reading purposes. But it was found that the library periods are only utilized by classes IV & V for the purpose of reading, as they are allowed to read and borrow library books. Children from classes I to III are not allowed to borrow books for home reading as they are thought to be very young and irresponsible, thus they might lose or damage the library books. Teachers raised the concern that children of classes I & II are not even allowed to read books in their library periods and therefore they only watch cartoons and documentary films on T.V. Because they think that this is the time when we need to develop reading habits, by teaching them how to handle books and be responsible. Thus untrained teachers in the sample school seemed to be unaware of the reading difficulties in children, their causes, and also of the remedial strategies for helping these children to overcome them. As a result, they were found to teach reading in different ways and not catering for the specific reading difficulties of children as identified by the Standardized tests.

However, reading specialists and trained reading teachers were found to be using a variety of remedial strategies to help children with reading difficulties as identified by Standardized assessment tests. The next section highlights the remedial strategies used by remedial centres to cater for the reading difficulties of the children.

Remedial Strategies

The test scores and trained reading teachers' interviews highlighted that children have reading difficulties. Hence teachers should be trained enough to deal with them. However, it was highlighted by the teachers that the theoretical aspect would not be enough; there should also be a practical aspect to it. For example,

> Only training is very abstract, you have to have internship with it. I don't
> think you can do it as a correspondence, I don't think you can just do it as
> a theory. There has to be a practical and really good understanding, unless
> you have diverse experience, which will help you understand this. (IST2)

It was also mentioned that early interventions help in the remediating process and therefore are found to have produced better results. As it was highlighted by the reading specialists' interviewed that the most important thing in the teaching and learning process is to be aware of the child's needs. Once teachers are aware of it then half of the problem is solved as this helps the child to be understood by the teachers. Therefore, early intervention is very important. It is the key to everything as the improvement is very prominent and incredible. Most research studies in literature also lay emphasis on early intervention to be the key to address reading problems (Snow, Burns & Griffin, 1998). Reading problems are preventable for the vast majority of students who encounter difficulty in learning to read, if these students receive extra support in the form of an early intervention program (Goldenberg, 1994; Hiebert & Taylor, 1994; Reynolds, 1991). Pikulski (1997) further concludes that every child has the right to develop into a thoughtful, competent reader.

One of the teachers expressed that, "learning how to read, write and spell is the most important thing … Early intervention, anything, which could start early, has the best prognosis." (IST2) Another teacher shared her insights by saying that:

> Usually you can pick these kids when they are in class one when they start to read and write. Because then you can identify the reading and writing problems. As these children are very bright, they know, they talk, they are so bright, they start writing that is the time when the child can be picked up, not before that. You see how you would know because they talk very bright. When they start reading and writing, then the problems arise. So you see before six they don't read and write so much because they do not have their motor development so much because how would you know if it is the hand control who is not doing it or is it the writing problems. (ITT1)

The remedial strategies found to be used by trained reading teachers were mainly based on phonic and multi-sensory approaches to teaching reading. One of the reading specialist teachers explained that a useful reading approach for helping these children is the multi-sensory approach as it is very well-structured; it uses the multi-sensory ways of teaching which stimulate all skills. It starts from very basis and builds up teaching directly the concepts in a very systematic way using all the modalities at the same time. The teachers try to teach the rules of phonics conceptually, by giving concrete examples of real life, which makes language learning interesting and effective for the children with reading difficulties. The relation to the child's daily life situations helps them to remember and recall. This also helps these children in the understanding the concepts of language learning for e.g. the way letters are matched with the sounds, mixing up different sounds to pronounce the words, breaking of the words into syllables, etc. which not only helps in reading, but also in writing and spellings.

The remedial strategies used to cater for children's reading difficulties are mostly based on the basic language skills and sub-skills, which are continuously drilled, reinforced and taught in a very slow and meaningful way. One of the remedial reading approaches which were used mostly in the remedial centres visited is the Orton-

Ghillingham Multi-Sensory Approach, as one of the reading specialist teachers using the Orton-Gillingham method explained that:

> It is a technique, which is devised to help kids with dyslexia or any learning disability. It's a multi-sensory teaching and the way you teach is the most important thing. So if I say like a digraph is a two consonants which go together to make one sound. I call it a digraph, you want to call it something else go ahead and do that. But the kids will pick up digraph. And I really explain the concept like h is a letter and s is a letter. And s and h get married. And s has got the sound ss and h has got the sound hh. But if they blend together they get something new, like s is the girl sally and h is harry. When they get married they give birth to a baby Sheela. It starts with the sound sh. So that concept can be explained in Urdu. So what my role is to make the kid understand that when s and h go together it is always sh. So you know that Orton-Gillingham has a very deep philosophy, it takes in the linguistic perspective, from speech point of view, from an education point of view, from a very research based technique. (IST2)

It was observed that the remediation has different levels. It starts from cards consisting of letters, which are divided into consonants and vowels. The child remembers the key words and the sounds attached to them. And if the child doesn't remember the sound, the word for e.g. umbrella is said, so he connects it with 'u'. It was highlighted in the interviews that the sound connection is very important. Sandpaper are also used to make them write, trace it out, trace it out in the air, so all the senses are used. Consonants and vowels are taken up one by one. Then they do have connecting exercises after every letter for the reinforcement of the letters taught. The lists of words which are given have connections with sounds and other letters learnt. The passage given also has connections with the same words. It was observed that the teacher taught the concept of diagraph by getting the child to mix blue and yellow colours. Then the teacher explained that, 's' has got a different sound and h has got a different sound, when they come together they make a new sound 'sh' (ITT1). So that is how the conceptual understanding is taught which the

57

child will never forget. Another example could be of diphthongs. The teacher explained that these are two vowels, which give one sound. Like ai –pail, sail, tail, ee-keep, sleep, oo-hook, shook, etc. and said that:

> For giving the concept of diphthongs, I have thought about diphthong is like a bird having two wings. With these two wings the bird can fly. Same way these are two diphthongs 'a' and 'i' like two wings and go together. If one is not there, the bird can't fly. Same is the case with the diphthongs; if they are not together it won't work. Both of them have to come together.
>
> (ITT1)

It was found during the interviews that several other methods are used for remedial training. However, they are mainly based on the multi-sensory approach. As one of the specialist teachers explained:

> We follow our own method which we have developed over these years. And we don't thrust a method on a child, we look at what the child's needs are and then we develop what he needs. Because you can realize that in reading, you can't do everything phonically, children may be very poor at auditory, some children are very poor at visual, it's a combination of the two that works the best. That is my research view, you have to have a phonic background, and you have to have a sight background, and you have to develop both, the visual-perception and auditory. So we do a lot of sub-skills with the children. You know a cross … visual to visual, auditory to auditory exercises, auditory to visual, visual to auditory, like showing the letters, asking to repeat what he saw, then showing the letters and asking to write what he saw, etc. a lot of activities are done all to facilitate reading. (IST1)

The teacher showed cards of alphabets, asking the children to read out the names, sounds and what they stand for. The children are engaged in different activities like circling the blends from the given words, multiple choice, fill in the blanks, sentence making, word formation, matching, etc. They are asked to pronounce the sounds, using their mouth and lips movements. It is also found that one of the remedial centres have their own special graded books for the children according to their own method of teaching, which may not be according to the grade level in schools.

It was observed that this remedial teaching is more effective when done on a one to one basis in order to cater for the individual difficulties and needs of the child. When children come to a level where they are at least able to read and write, then the remedial teaching can be done in small groups also. However, it seems that the teachers can also use these remedial teaching strategies for the whole class, to address their children's learning needs in a more meaningful way. One of the teachers emphasized that reading difficulties can only be dealt with individually, thus reading is not to be remediated in a group but has to be done on one to one basis. (IST1) The remedial session observed was conducted by the specialist and trained reading teachers with a small group of four students or individually. It was observed that the teacher catered for the individual needs and gave individual attention according to the level of the students. (RO1) Literature also supports remedial teaching on a one to one basis or in small groups in order to help the children's reading difficulties with coping strategies to facilitate their learning process (Kunc, 1992; Slavin, 1995; William, 1990; CEC Today, 1997). However, one of the reading specialists was not in the favour of taking these children out of the mainstream classrooms throughout their schooling years but only for extra help at times of need. She explained this view point as follows:

> Yes, they should be a part of the mainstream classrooms. But the thing is that sometimes they do require special school because it depends upon what kind of learning disability you have. Then you know it is difficult to remediate, they won't be able to function in the regular classroom and may be they need to be pulled out for a couple of years and then mainstream. But that is where they belong. (IST2)

Access and availability of remedial teaching

One of the specialist teachers claimed that they were providing trained teachers to the schools around. These teachers could prove to be better classroom teachers in the schools as they had been trained. However, it seems that the remedial centres are only catering to the needs of children in a few high-income schools, as their services are very expensive. Even the teacher training course they offer is very expensive. So only the rich people could get access to their services that could afford their fees. A specialist teacher while justifying the high fees explained how they try to make their services accessible to children from poor families:

> We are very expensive; there is no doubt because special education is very expensive. All the material, all the tests we get from abroad which cost the earth. They are very, very expensive. So we do… and we are not a funded institute, so we have to pay for our own rent and everything from the what ever we make. But inspite of all that we never refuse anybody. Who ever come, what we do is we don't provide free services. We ask the parents how much you can pay, a thousand or five hundred or what ever, rest we try and get a sponsorship so that the institute doesn't suffer and the teachers who do a lot of work, they should also get their remediation. Because it is very important for parents to feel like they have self pride. (IST1)

But still one of the trained teacher felt that she could not refer parents to these remedial centres as they are very expensive: "I can't also ask my parents to go to these remedial centres because they are very expensive and the parents can't afford their fees" (ITT1).

Strategies for creating awareness amongst the untrained reading teachers and parents

It was found that children with reading difficulties are referred to the remedial centres by the nearby schools, which seemed to be aware of their services. Some of the parents also play the role of spreading the awareness by referring other unaware parents, whose children have problems in learning. As one of the teachers said:

> Mostly these children are identified in the schools, or sometimes by the parents also. Sometimes the doctors also send children to us, the neurologist or someone's friend's child is coming here, refer them. But it is very difficult because Karachi is huge place; we are situated in a place,

60

which is very difficult to access, where accessibility is very difficult. (IST1)

Remedial centres also conduct workshops and have open houses for spreading awareness among the people. As a proprietor of a remedial centre explained:

Apart from doing the course, our second task, which is a very important task, is of creating awareness. For this we have open house at our institute, we call speakers, we show films. We have had two very successful open houses for the school teachers from various schools. It is very difficult, I agree to get teachers to everybody but now we find that they are more students than they were fourteen years ago. It is not that suddenly everyone is becoming learning disabled; it is because the awareness has increased. People are more aware now so they would like something to be done with their children. (IST1)

The reading specialists highlighted the importance of counseling parents and teachers of these children to facilitate their learning process at home and in the school. One of them expressed that, "I can't really do intervention work if I don't do parent counseling. We counsel teachers at schools, counsel people who are even helping at the school level, and I counsel parents who are helping at home and then ourselves. So it's a triangle" (IST2). It seems that these children need more attention, time and encouragement by their teachers, peers and parents so that their confidence can be built up. As one of the trained teachers expressed:

The most important thing that these children require is more time. You see what happens is that they are slow, because they cannot read, they cannot write, they cannot comprehend, etc. as compared to the rest of the class which is going at a certain pace. And they feel overwhelmed. It just feels like a big wave is coming and crushes them. It is very important that their self-esteem is not hurt, and they should not be labeled. They need more understanding from their parents at home and their peers, and their teachers also, and they just need more time and building up their self-image and motivating techniques, and you know what really works for these younger kids is a token reward system. You keep giving the stars and crosses and very goods and lots of excellent. Just keep on encouraging them and that really works. It is just that the teacher had to be understanding, has patience and friendly attitude and really wants to help these children and this will work magic for those children. (ITT2)

It seems that the remedial strategies used for dealing with children's reading difficulties in schools and remedial centres are mainly phonic and multi-sensory approaches, whereas the reading programs implemented in the sample school, emphasized on the whole language approach. In addition to the above mentioned approaches, the interviews with the specialist reading teachers highlighted the basal and linguistic approaches are used for the purpose of teaching reading in some schools. It seems that we need to look beyond the strategies that are already being used in schools for teaching reading effectively. Literature also highlights the merits and demerits of the above mentioned approaches of teaching reading, especially benefits of phonic approach have been found in research also. Over 180 research studies have proven that phonics is the best and the only way to teach reading to students having dyslexia (Child Development Institute, 1997). But 80% of the schools do not use an intensified phonics approach for reading instruction. They use the whole word - see and say approach or a cursory use of phonics along with the whole word method - word pictures and guessing. As compared to whole language approach, research shows that the phonemic approach can facilitate effective reading acquisition as over 180 research studies to date have proven that phonics is the only best way to teach reading to all the students, especially students with reading difficulties (Shaywitz, 1996c).

In addition, literature also highlights that 80% of the schools do not use an intensified phonics approach for reading instruction. As Cramer (1996) explains that phonetic approach focuses instruction on learning to associate printed letters and combinations of letters with their corresponding errors, whereas whole language approach is based on the understanding that reading is finding the meaning in written

62

language. He further claims that a balanced approach to teaching reading combines a strong foundation in phonics with whole language methods. Therefore, teachers need to be aware of the instructional activities that can help the students to become aware of phonemes before they receive formal reading instruction. They also need to realize that phonemic awareness will become more sophisticated as the students' reading skills develop (Lundberg et al., 1988). According to Yopp (1992), phonemic awareness is both a prerequisite for and a consequence of learning to read. Phonological awareness significantly improves a child's ability to read (Bradley & Bryant, 1985, Shaywitz, 1996b). Its role in beginning reading has the potential to support both the extremes of the whole language vs. phonics debate over reading instruction. According to Griffith & Olson (1992), regardless of instructional technique, phonological awareness is an essential element for reading progress. In another study, Griffith et al., (1992) found that children with high phonemic awareness outperformed those with low phonemic awareness on all literacy measures, whether they were taught using a whole language approach or traditional basal instruction.

However, Adams (1990) argues that phonemic approach supporters need to admit that teaching students letter-sound correspondences is meaningless if they do not have a solid visual familiarity with the individual letters and if they do not understand that the sounds paired with those letters are what make up words. Research evidence does not support the use of 'whole language' reading approaches to teach dyslexic children. It has repeatedly demonstrated that lack of phonemic awareness is the root cause of reading failure. Reading failure caused by dyslexia is highly preventable through direct, explicit instruction in phonemic awareness. On the one hand, phonemic awareness is the most important core and causal factor separating normal and disabled readers. On the other hand, lack of phonemic awareness is the most powerful determinant of failure to learn to read (CEC Today, 1997; Bright Solutions for dyslexia, 1998). Honig (1996) offers a review of reading research supporting a balanced approach and presents detailed guidelines on how to integrate whole language principles with the necessary foundation reading skills. Perhaps a new approach, which has a combination of a variety of activities from different approaches, can be effective which could cater to the child's needs. The researchers' point of view on the strategies used for preventing and correcting reading difficulties, is that it should be explicit, have systematic instruction, guided by on-going assessment including teaching approaches related to multi-sensory methods like the Orton-Gillingham approach, etc. Research reveals that the most useful interventions for reading difficulties consist of a combination of explicit and direct instruction in phonemic awareness, sound-symbol relationships (phonics), and contextual reading and reading comprehension skills.

Chapter Five

CONCLUSION

This chapter summarizes the major findings from the research study conducted to identify 'children's reading difficulties' in English at the primary level in the multi-lingual context of Pakistan where English is a second, third or foreign language. The aim of the study was to identify children's reading difficulties and to explore facilities available to deal with these problems. This chapter also highlights the issues and the challenges raised in the research study, followed by some recommendations in order to help the teachers and schools in dealing with children's reading difficulties.

Major Findings and Issues

The major findings of the research study are as follows:

- The untrained reading teachers were not aware of the specific reading difficulties and did not have the skills and resources either to identify children's reading difficulties or to cater for the same.

- The common reading problems identified by those teachers related to the mechanics of reading like pronunciation problems, word recognition, vocabulary and comprehension problems. In contrast, both the specialist reading teachers in the remedial centres and trained reading teachers working in some selected schools, highlighted specific reading difficulties in children such as reversals, omissions, substitutions, deletions, repetitions and comprehension problems.

- Reading was taught by drilling, reading aloud and silent reading in the school by these 'untrained' reading teachers. In addition, different reading programs such as Oxford Reading Tree and Ginn Reading Program were used in the school. However, remedial centres teach reading through phonic and multi-sensory approaches like Orton Ghillingham approach, Horns Bee approach, etc.

- Standardized tests for identifying reading difficulties in children were found to be inappropriate for children whose first (and often even second) language is not English. This raises the issue of the validity of the tests' scores. Consequently the results of the tests conducted during the study were interpreted with caution.

- Assessing reading difficulties and implementing remedial strategies need specialized training. Therefore an untrained teacher cannot use the assessment instruments to identify children's reading difficulties and also needs training and understanding for implementing remedial strategies.
- The major causes highlighted by the teachers for these reading difficulties in children are inappropriate and inadequate teaching of reading, lack of language exposure and reading culture, lack of supportive learning environment, bi-lingual and multi-lingual context.
- The teachers working in remedial centres and selected schools remediate the children with reading difficulties on a one to one basis or in small groups giving individual attention to cater for the needs accordingly. Also in a few schools, a pull-out program is implemented where the children with reading difficulties are pulled out from the classroom and are given remedial help in their free periods, or in music, P.T and art periods.
- The schools presently dealing with children's reading difficulties are very few in number (five). Moreover, these are high standard schools for the elite class only.
- Remedial centres are also very few in number (four) and therefore expensive. Thus very few people can afford to use their services. The teacher training programs offered by these remedial centres are also very expensive.

The issues raised from the study's findings were that children have reading difficulties but in majority of the schools, the teachers are unaware and untrained, therefore are not catering for the same. This was also found in the sample school where the needs analysis was done, that the teachers were not conversant with the reading difficulties as they were not aware and therefore were not doing anything to help the learning process of these children. The awareness level seems to range from lack of awareness to a high level of awareness and that has to do with the socio-economic level of the society as there are remedial centres and few elite schools which do cater for children's reading and other learning problems but only inclusive to the rich and high income class. The main issue raised is that there are limited facilities available, which are very expensive and therefore can only cater for the children's needs of elite class whose parents' income level is high. And, even if remedial facilities are available in certain schools, they are again for that particular class of schools (i.e. for elite class children). Is it suitable and effective to refer children from a low socio-economic background to these remedial centres and schools which are very expensive? Or can this awareness be spread where teachers could do something in the schools?

One of the main issues highlighted in the interviews, was that the teaching of reading is not done appropriately and therefore the teachers suggested that they should be trained for teaching of reading in a systematic way. It seems that the teaching of reading is not given importance as more emphasis is given to written work than to reading in schools as well as at home because of the written examinations. The school has to acknowledge that there is a problem in assessment, as reading skills are not assessed. Testing would be useful in this area, in identifying the specific reading difficulties in children because the sample children who were assessed in this research study were diagnosed to some extent having reading difficulties. Even though it was a very small sample it was nevertheless, a representative sample, randomly picked up from the class. And therefore, if there is a problem, it needs to be addressed.

The major issue identified by the untrained reading teachers was the identification of children's specific reading difficulties. It requires training; however, even after the training it was found that the trained teachers were not in a position to use the assessment tools. Even there are no local tests available. Tests that are available are standardized for a native English population and not accessible as they have copyrights. As conducting these tests needs specialized training, they are also time consuming and the results too, are not valid as English is the second, third or a foreign language in this multi-lingual context of Pakistan. Therefore the major issue for the untrained reading teachers, who really want to help children, is how to identify and remediate children's reading difficulties. However, the reading difficulties identified by conducting the Standardized tests could be owing to lack of language exposure, as English is not a native language for the children. The types of errors made by the children in the tests and the causes identified by the teacher highlighted an important issue; whether these difficulties are because of dis-functioning of the brain or are ESL/EFL problems? Therefore, it was suggested by the teachers interviewed that if children are given exposure to supportive language learning environment in a multi-lingual context, than there might be no problems at all.

Challenges

The following were the major challenges faced during the research study:

Unfamiliarity of the topic and lack of support

I was interested in "children's reading difficulties" in English, therefore, I chose to work on this topic to enhance my own learning while conducting my research study. Since the topic was new to me, I had to do a lot of independent study. Often it was very difficult for me to understand some of the technical terms and explanation while reading the literature available. Again it was very challenging for me to relate my reading to the multi-lingual context of Pakistan where English is not a native language. I faced a lot of problems during my research work, as the topic was unfamiliar but more importantly, there was no faculty at IED with a specialization in this field. Even in the M.Ed. program, there was little exposure to the issues involved in learning and reading difficulties.

Non-availability of local tests

It was found that some testing tools have been developed in Pakistan, but are still in the mode of testing for validity. So there were no local tests available. Therefore I had to use Standardized tests which have been developed for native speakers. Consequently, the results had to be interpreted with caution.

Challenges in conducting and assessing Standardized tests

The accessibility of the standardized tests was again a problem, as the tests were expensive and had copyrights. Moreover, I was not trained to conduct these tests. Thus I had to request a clinical psychologist to help me in identifying, conducting and analyzing the tests. The tests conducted in the school to identify children's reading difficulties consumed a lot of time as they were conducted both individually and in-groups. I had to rely on the resource person throughout the process of conducting the tests in the school, scoring of the test results and analyzing the errors made by the students to interpret the types of reading difficulties children have. Due to the prior commitments of the resource person at her own work place, it took us a considerably longer time to conduct the tests and interpret the results. This affected greatly the timelines of my study.

Refocusing of the Study

As mentioned above, due to not being trained, I faced challenges in conducting the Standardized tests. I initially planned for an intervention in phase II of the research work. But it was found that one also needs to be trained or get help from an educational psychologist, who could then help in remediating, the identified reading problem. But because of this I had to refocus the study from an intervention phase to an exploration one where I visited, interviewed, and observed specialist and trained reading teachers in the remedial centres and other schools which are catering for the children's reading difficulties.

Recommendations

To address the above mentioned issues faced during the research study, the following recommendations are made to highlight the possibilities available for teachers and schools to cater for children's reading difficulties in multi-lingual school contexts in Pakistan:

Appropriate teaching of reading by the teachers

Reading should be taught in an appropriate way. Even if the children do not have specific reading difficulties, the teaching of reading should be done in an effective way by using approaches like the phonic approach and the multi-sensory approach, which are well structured approaches for teaching of reading. For this teachers should be given training in teaching reading effectively. This will not only benefit the children having reading difficulties but will also help other children to learn reading skills effectively. Therefore, the teaching of reading should be taken as a priority skill in the language development of children at the primary level.

Raising teachers' awareness level through workshops and training programs

It is recommended to raise the teachers' awareness level through workshops and training programs conducted by professionals in this field, so that the teachers are at least aware of the problem and can therefore help the children with a positive attitude. The teachers should at least be alerted to the kinds of symptoms in children with reading difficulties. Thus, in addition to their teaching experiences and monitoring of the students' work and performance in the classroom can help teachers in identifying children with severe reading difficulties. Then the identified children could be sent to the specialist reading teachers or to remedial centres for specific assessment of the nature and severity of the problem. As a result, these children can be helped accordingly in the class during the school timings as well as through a pull out program or after school hours. IED and other educational training institutions should also offer workshops and training programs in the field of special education. IED should also support future research study in this area.

Provisions and facilities provided by the school to cater for children's reading difficulties

The school should have some kind of a policy in place to enable the teachers to implement what they have learnt through special training programs. For e.g. for one to one remedial teaching or a pull out program, the school must have provisions and facilities to accommodate these strategies to work effectively. In addition, guidelines need to be prepared regarding the policy, resources required for the identification of reading difficulties, assessment process and tools used, remedial training and counseling of the parents. The school will have to have some kind of policy where teachers can refer children to remedial centres, which are catering for the reading difficulties of the children and share expenses with parents who cannot afford to pay for the remedial services in these centres. However, it would be more useful if one or more teachers in a school are or school systems do send teachers for training as reading teachers. These teachers can then be entrusted with the role of helping teachers in their school or school system both with identification of reading difficulties in children as well as remedial training of children with severe problems in reading.

Some type of inventory or a checklist could be developed for initial identification of the learning problems of the children in specific language areas like reading, writing, listening, speaking, and other areas which could identify the child's strengths and weaknesses. Gardners' multiple intelligence theory could be a good way of highlighting children's areas of strengths and weaknesses.

To help the teachers identify the child's learning problems and to monitor the progress of each child, a child's learning profile should be developed. In addition to the checklist inventory, this will help the teachers in becoming aware of children's learning styles, work level, classroom participation, etc. and building effectively on their existing strengths and weaknesses.

Special training for the teachers and development of a resource unit at the school or at the system level

The reading teacher who has received a specialist training can then work with a number of classes and teachers in the school, and help in conducting remedial programs. Therefore, a specialist attached with the school to help to remediate this problem. The identified children by the teachers could then be sent to these specialist reading teachers or to the remedial centres for specific assessment, which could then thoroughly identify the severity and the nature of the problem in order to remediate and help the child accordingly in the class as well as in the remedial centre or a pull out program during the school timings or after the school. Special training for the teachers and then working in a special resource unit with other teachers in the schools could help in catering for reading difficulties of children by conducting remedial programs. Also the reading teachers can work together to conduct seminars and workshops for other teachers and parents for awareness raising and training to help in the dealing of this problem.

Awareness raising for parents by seminars and workshops

Parents and guardians are often unaware of their child's problems at school. Seminars and workshops should be conducted in order to make the parents aware of these problems so that they have a change in their attitude and become a supporting factor along with the teachers to help the child to overcome these difficulties.

Change in teachers' attitude to build up the child's self-esteem and confidence

The teacher should have a positive attitude towards these children, give them more time, give concessions and facilitate their learning process by not penalizing them to perform above the level of which they are capable. Teachers should also be appreciative of their efforts and develop an understanding of the problem to help children in building up their self-esteem and confidence to achieve success in learning.

Developing local tests for the identification of reading difficulties

Some tests are being developed in Urdu for the identifying children's reading difficulties in Pakistan but still they are in the phase of validity testing. It is recommended that local tests should be developed in both Urdu as well as English as reading difficulties are generally found across languages.

Lesson Learnt

As I was unfamiliar and untrained in this field of special education, 'reading difficulties in children,' I learned a lot by reading literature while exploring the topic during my research study. As a teacher I learnt about different types of reading difficulties of children and their causes, specially the reasons for reading difficulties of children in English as a second or foreign language and a multi-lingual context. While conducting the research study I interviewed 'untrained' teachers, specialist and trained reading teachers and also observed their reading and remedial lessons. The study gave me opportunities to explore the facilities available in the remedial centres and think about what can be done in the school context where the need analysis was done in the first phase of this study.

The study gave me an in-depth understanding of how as a teacher, I could help children with reading difficulties in my classroom and also as a teacher educator, work with other teachers and parents to raise their awareness level. Also it highlighted the need for arranging special training workshops and programs for teachers who are interested in this area so that they can become trained reading teachers in the schools and can then establish a resource unit for the school system, to help children with reading difficulties.

REFERENCES

Adams, M. J. (1990). <u>Beginning to read: Thinking and learning about print.</u>
    Cambridge, MA: Bolt, Berannek, and Newman, Inc.

Antonoff, S. J. (1998). <u>Dyslexia and other learning disabilities signs and signals: A text</u>
    <u>for attorneys in the juvenile justice system.</u> New York: The International Dyslexia
    Association.

Beech, J. R. (1985). <u>Learning to read: A cognitive approach to reading and poor reading.</u>
    Great Britain: Biddles Ltd.

Brescia, W. & Fortune, J. C. (1988). Standardized testing of American Indian students.
    [On line] Available: http:///www.ed.gov/databases/ERIC_Digests/ed296813.html

Bright Solutions for Dyslexia. (1998). [On line] Available: Email:brightsol@aol.com

Bryant, P. & Bradley, L. (1985). <u>Children's reading problems: Psychology & education.</u>
    U.S.A: Blackwell.

CEC Today. (1997). Reading difficulties vs. Learning disabilities. A publication of the
    council for exceptional children. <u>CEC Today, 4 </u>(5), pp.1-3.

Child Development Institute. (1997). About dyslexia and reading problems. [On line]
    Available: http://childdevelopmentinfo.com/learning/dyslexia.html

Council for learning disabilities (CLD). (1997). Infosheet: What do we know about the
    characteristics of learning disabilities? [On line] Available:
    http://www.winthrop.edu./cld/Infosheet%20Characteristics.html

Cotterell, G.C. (1980). Diagnosis in the classroom. The centre for the teaching of reading. School of education. University of reading. Suffolk School Psychological Service.

Cramer, S. (1996). How children learn to read: 'Building blocks of reading.' [On line] Available: http://www.Idonline.org/Id_indepth/reading/ccld_learn.html

Crombie, M. A. (1997). The effects of specific learning difficulties (dyslexia) on the learning of a foreign language in school. Dyslexia, 3, pp.27-47.

Crowder, R. G. & Wagner, R. K. (1992). The psychology of reading: An introduction. 2nd edition. New York: Oxford University Press.

Dockrell, J., & McShane, J. (1992). Children's learning difficulties: A cognitive approach. U.S.A: Blackwell.

Essential Learning Institute. (1995). Beginning reading and phonological awareness for students with learning disabilities. [On line] Available: http://rsts.net/eli/articles/readers.html

Favreau, M., Komoda, M. K. & Segalowitz, N. (1980). Second language reading: Implications of the word superiority effect in skilled bilinguals. Canadian Journal of Psychology, 34, pp.370-380.

Frost, J. A. & Emery, M. J. (1995). Academic interventions for dyslexic children with phonological core deficits. [On line] Available: http://www.ed.gov/databases/ERIC-Digests/edED385095.html

Gaffney, J. S. (1998). The prevention of reading failure: Teach reading and writing. In J. Osborn & F. Lehr (Eds.). Literacy for all: Issues in teaching and learning. New York: Guilford Publications, Inc. [On line] Available: http://www.guilford.com/frameexc.html

Goldenberg, C. (1994). Promoting early literacy development among Spanish speaking children: Lessons from two studies. In E. H. Hiebert & B. M. Taylor (Eds.). Getting reading right from the start. (pp.171-200). Boston, M.A: Allyn & Bacon.

Griffith, P. et al. (1992). The effect of phonemic awareness on the literacy development of first grade children in a traditional or a whole language classroom. Journal of Research in Childhood Education, 6 (2), pp.85-92.

Griffith, P. & Olson. M. W. (1992). Phonemic awareness helps beginning readers break the code. Reader Teacher, 45 (7), pp.516-523.

Gupta, R. M. & Coxhead, P. (1990). Intervention with children. London: Routledge.

Guron, L.M. & Lundberg, I. (2000). Dyslexia and second language reading: A second bite at the apple? Reading and Writing: An Interdisciplinary journal, 12 (1-2), pp. 41-61.

Hastings, R. P., Hewes, A., Lock, S. & Witting, A. (1996). Do special education needs courses have any impact on student teachers' perceptions of children with severe learning difficulties? British journal of special education, 23(3), pp. 139-144.

Hiebert, E. H. & Taylor, B. M. (1994). Getting reading right from the start. Boston: Allyn & Bacon.

Hoein, T. & Lundberg,I. (1997). Dysleksi: Fra teoritil praksis [Dyslexia: from theory to practice]. Oslo: Ad Notam Gyldendal.

Honig, B. (1996). Teaching our children to read: The role of skills in a comprehensive reading program. Thousand Oaks, CA: Corwin Press.

Hornsby, B. (1984). <u>Overcoming dyslexia: A straightforward guide for families and teachers.</u> Ontario: Prentice-Hall Canada Inc.

Jackson, N. E. & Roller, C. M. (1993). Reading with young children. [On line] Available: <u>http://www.gifted.uconn.edu/jackroll.html</u>

Judah, B. A. (1999). The many facets of dyslexia. [On line]Available: WORLDWORKSWorldworks@lifematters.com

Kunc, N. (1992). The need to belong: Rediscovering Maslow's hierarchy of needs. In R. Villa, J. Thousand, W. Stainback, & S. Stainback (Eds.). <u>Restructuring for caring & effective education.</u> Baltimove: Paul Brookes.

Lacey, P. & Porter, J. (1996). Enabling teachers in-service education in learning difficulties and challenging behaviour. <u>Journal of in-service education, 24</u> (3), pp.475-489.

Larcombe, T. (1985). <u>Mathematical learning difficulties in the secondary school: Pupils' needs and teacher roles.</u> The Open University: Milton Keynes.

Leadbetter, J. & Leadbetter, P. (1993). <u>Special children: Meeting the challenge in the primary school.</u> London: Cassell.

Lerner, J. W. (1989). <u>Learning disabilities: Theories, diagnosis, and teaching strategies.</u> U.S.A: Houghton Mifflin Company.

Lerner, J. W. (1996). New study on teaching of reading: Preventing reading difficulties in young children. [On line] Available: <u>http://www.Idonline.org./Id_indepth/reading/nrc-lerner.html</u>

Lewkowicz, M. D. (1996). Testing for assessment of a reading problem. [On line] Available: http://www.kidsource.com/LDA-CA/reading.html

Lokerson, J. (1992a). Learning disabilities: Glossary of some important terms. [On line]Available: http://www.ed.gov/databases/ERIC-Digests/edED352780.html

Lokerson, J. (1992b). Learning disabilities. [On line] Available: http://www.ed.gov/databases/ERIC-Digests/edED352779.html

Lundberg, I. et al. (1988). Effectiveness of an extensive program for stimulating phonological awareness in preschool children. Reading Research Quarterly, 23 (3), pp.263-284.

McGuinness, D. (1997). Why children can't read: And what we can do about it. England: Penguin Books.

Menyuk, P. (1996). Early ways to predict poor readers. [On line] Available: http://www.kidsource.com/ASHA/poorread.html

Osmond, J. (1993). The reality of dyslexia. London: Cassell.

Pikulski, J. J. (1997). Preventing reading problems: Factors common to successful early intervention programs. [On line] Available: http://eduplace.com/rdg/res/prevent.html

Pollock, J. & Waller, E. (1997). Day-to-day dyslexia in the classroom. London: Routledge.

Pressley, M. (1998). Reading instruction that works: The case for balanced teaching: Children who experience problems in learning to read. [On line] Available: http://www.guilford.com/frameexc.html

Pumfrey, P. & Delliot, C. (1993). <u>Children's difficulties in reading, spelling and writing.</u> London: The Falmer Press.

Ramey, P. E. (1998). Brain structure may play role in children's ability to learn to read. [On line] Available: <u>HYPERLINK</u> <u>http://www.sciencedaily.com/releases/1998/11/981104092933 html</u>

Reynolds, A. J. (1991). Early schooling of children at risk. <u>American educational research journal, 28.</u> pp. 3392-422.

River, J. E. (1999). Reading news "We have found a piece to the puzzle" Reading problems solved! [On line] Available: <u>http://www.neuro.read.net</u>

Root, C. (1994). A guide to learning disabilities for the ESL classroom practitioner. [On line] Available: <u>http://www.Idonline.org/ld_indepth/bilingual_ld/esl_ld.html</u>

Schwarz, R. (1995). ESL instruction for learning disabled adults. [On line] Available: <u>http://www.nche.gwu.edu/library/specialed.html</u>

Segalowitz, N. (1986). Skilled reading in the second language. In J. Vaid, (Ed.), <u>Language processing in bilinguals: Psycholinguisticand neurological perspectives.</u> pp.3-19, Hillsdale, NJ: Erlbaum.

Sensenbaugh, R. (1995). Phonemic awareness: An important early step in learning to read. [On line] Available: <u>http://www.ed.gov/databases/ERIC-Digests/edED400530.html</u>

Shaywitz, S. (1996a). Dyslexia: 10 years of brain imaging research shows the brain reads sound by sound. [On line] Available: <u>http://childdevelopmentinfo.com/learning/brain.html</u>

Shaywitz, S. E. (1996b). Dyslexia. Scientific American. [On line] Available: http://childdevelopmentinfo.com/learning/brain.html

Shaywitz, S. (1996c). Improving reading for children and teens. [On line] Available: http://childdevelopment info.com/learning/improving_reading.shtml#Top

Shimon, J. & Sivan, T. (1994). Reading proficiency and orthography: Evidence from Hebrew and English. Language learning, 44, pp.5-27.

Slavin, R. E. (1995). Neverstreaming: Ending learning disabilities before they start. [On line]Available: http://www.newhorizons.org

Smith, C. R. (1991). Learning disabilities: The interaction of learner, task and setting. Boston: Allyn & Bacon.

Smith, C. A. (1992). Helping children overcome reading difficulties. [On line] Available: http://www.ed.gov/databases/ERIC-Digests/edED344190.html

Snow, C.E., Burns, M.S. & Griffins, P. (1998). Preventing reading difficulties in young children. [On line] Available: http://www.nap.edu/readingroom/books/prdyc/index.html

Spolsky, B. (1989). Conditions for second language learning. Oxford: Oxford University Press.

TeachEach (1997). What is a learning disability? [On line] Available: http://www.schwablearning.org

Teachers' Resource Centre (TRC) Workshop Handout C # 532. (2000). Diagnosing dyslexia: Understanding psychoeducational assessment. Presented by: Ms. Mahjabeen Sidik, Center for Assessment and Remedial Education (CARE).

The National Centre for Learning Disabilities, the Orton Dyslexia Society & the Learning Disabilities Association of America. (1996). What teachers can do about learning disabilities. [On line] Available: http://Idoline.org/Id_indepth/teaching_teachiniques/teaching-1.html

Turnbull, A., Turnbull, R., Shank, M. & Leal, D. (1999). Exceptional lives: Special education in today's schools. (2nd edition). U.S.A: Merrill.

University of Washington. (1999). Dyslexia children use nearly five times the brain to perform an ordinary language task as normal children. [On line] Available: http://www.washington.edu/newsroom/news/1999archive/10-99archive/k1000499.html

Vito, P. (1991). On standardized testing. [On line] Available: http://www.ed.gov/databases/ERIC_Digests/ed338445.html

Vellutino, F. R. (1987). Dyslexia. Scientific American, 256(3), pp. 34–41.

Webb, G. M. (1992). Needless battles on dyslexia. Education week, 32.

William, P. (1990). Children with learning difficulties. In N. Entwistle, (Ed.) Handbook of Educational Ideas & Practices. New York: Routledge.

Winebrenner, S. (1996). Teaching kids with learning difficulties in regular classroom: Strategies and techniques every teacher can use to challenge and motivate struggling students. U.S.A: Free Spirit Publishing Inc.

Yopp, H. K. (1992). Developing phonemic awareness in young children. Reading Teacher, 45 (9), pp.696-703.